P9-CJH-182

Beyond
Baby Talk

Beyond Baby Talk

From Sounds to Sentences—
A Parent's Complete Guide to
Language Development

Kenn Apel, Ph.D., CCC-SLP

Julie J. Masterson, Ph.D., CCC-SLP

Sponsored by The American
Speech-Language-Hearing Association

PRIMA PUBLISHING
3000 Lava Ridge Court • Roseville, California 95661
(800) 632-8676 • www.primalifestyles.com

© 2001 by Kenn Apel and Julie Masterson

All rights reserved. No part of this book may be reproduced or transmitted in any form or by any means, electronic or mechanical, including photocopying, recording, or by any information storage or retrieval system, without written permission from Prima Publishing, except for the inclusion of brief quotations in a review.

PRIMA PUBLISHING and colophon are trademarks of Prima Communications Inc., registered with the United States Patent and Trademark Office.

Photos on pages 24, 73, 94, 112, and 121 courtesy of Alice Cabrera Elspas. Other photos courtesy of PhotoDisc.

Library of Congress Cataloging-in-Publication Data
Apel, Kenn
    Beyond Baby Talk : from sounds to sentences: a parent's complete guide to language development / Kenn Apel, Julie Masterson
        p.   cm.
    Includes bibliographical references and index.
    ISBN 0-7615-2647-1
    1. Children—Language. 2. Language acquisition. I. Apel, Kenn. II. Title.
LB1139.L3 M245   2001
372.6—dc21   2001033932

01 02 03 04 HH 10 9 8 7 6 5 4 3 2 1
Printed in the United States of America

How to Order
Single copies may be ordered from Prima Publishing, 3000 Lava Ridge Court, Roseville, CA 95661; telephone (800) 632-8676. Quantity discounts are also available. On your letterhead, include information concerning the intended use of the books and the number of books you wish to purchase.

Visit us online at www.primalifestyles.com

To Lynda and Jerry,
for their love and support,
and to our children,
for bringing joy and wonder to our life's work

CONTENTS

How Does Your Child

Hearing and Understanding

Yes / No

Birth–3 Months

- Startles to loud sounds.
- Quiets or smiles when spoken to.
- Seems to recognize your voice and quiets if crying.
- Increases or decreases sucking behavior in response to sound.

4–6 Months

- Moves eyes in direction of sounds.
- Responds to changes in tone of your voice.
- Notices toys that make sounds.
- Pays attention to music.

7 Months–1 Year

- Enjoys games like peek-a-boo and pat-a-cake.
- Turns and looks in direction of sounds.
- Listens when spoken to.
- Recognizes words for common items like "cup," "shoe," "juice."
- Begins to respond to requests ("Come here," "Want more?").

Yes / No

1–2 Years

- Points to a few body parts when asked.
- Follows simple commands and understands simple questions ("Roll the ball," "Kiss the baby," "Where's your shoe?").
- Listens to simple stories, songs, and rhymes.
- Points to pictures in a book when named.

2–3 Years

- Understands differences in meaning ("go-stop," "in-on," "big-little," "up-down").
- Follows two requests ("Get the book and put it on the table").

3–4 Years

- Hears you when you call from another room.
- Hears television or radio at the same loudness level as other family members.
- Answers simple "who?," "what?," "where?," "why?" questions.

4–5 Years

- Pays attention to a short story and answers simple questions about it.
- Hears and understands most of what is said at home and in school.

Instructions: Read each statement for your child's age group and check yes or no.

Every child is unique and has an individual rate of development. This chart represents, on average, the age by which most children will accomplish the listed skills. Children typically do not master all items in a category until they reach the upper age in each age range. Just because your child has not accomplished one skill within an age range does not mean the child has a disorder. However, if you have answered no to the majority of items in an age range, seek the advice of an ASHA-certified speech-language pathologist or audiologist.

© American Speech-Language-Hearing Association • www.asha.org

Hear and Talk?

Yes / No

Birth–3 Months
- Makes pleasure sounds (cooing, gooing).
- Cries differently for different needs.
- Smiles when sees you.

4–6 Months
- Babbling sounds more speech-like with *many* different sounds, including *p, b,* and *m.*
- Vocalizes excitement and displeasure.
- Makes gurgling sounds when left alone and when playing with you.

7 Months–1 Year
- Babbling has both long and short groups of sounds such as "tata upup bibibibi."
- Uses speech or non-crying sounds to get and keep attention.
- Imitates different speech sounds.
- Has 1 or 2 words (bye-bye, dada, mama) although they may not be clear.

1–2 Years
- Says more words every month.
- Uses some 1–2-word questions ("where kitty?" "go bye-bye?" "what's that?").
- Puts 2 words together ("more cookie," "no juice," "mommy book").
- Uses many different consonant sounds at the beginning of words.

Yes / No

2–3 Years
- Has a word for almost everything.
- Uses 2–3-words to talk about and ask for things.
- Speech is understood by familiar listeners most of the time.
- Often asks for or directs attention to objects by naming them.

3–4 Years
- Talks about activities at school or at friends' homes.
- People outside family usually understand child's speech.
- Uses a lot of sentences that have 4 or more words.
- Usually talks easily without repeating syllables or words.

4–5 Years
- Voice sounds clear like other children's.
- Uses sentences that give lots of details (e.g., "I like to read my books").
- Tells stories that stick to topic.
- Communicates easily with other children and adults.
- Says most sounds correctly except a few like *l, s, r, v, z, j, ch, sh, th.*
- Uses the same grammar as the rest of the family.

ACKNOWLEDGMENTS

We would like to thank Frederick T. Spahr, Executive Director of the American Speech-Language-Hearing Association (ASHA) and Joanne K. Jessen, ASHA Director of Publications, for asking us to participate in this project and for their support throughout the process. We are also grateful to Janet Gallant for her guidance and input in the initial stages of this book's proposal and to Vicki Deal-Williams and Silvia Martinez of ASHA's Office of Multicultural Affairs for their helpful information on bilingualism and dialect and other issues covered in our chapter "The Influence of Culture on Language." Special thanks are extended to Jamie Miller of Prima Publishing for her editorial assistance. Finally, we wish to acknowledge all of the researchers in child language, especially Margaret Lahey, whose work has been particularly influential on us.

INTRODUCTION

Your Best Tool: Knowing About Language

DID YOU KNOW?

- Parents are the primary "language role models" for their children.

- Language involves more than just a child's vocabulary. It involves the sounds we use, the sentences we make, and the way we use language to get what we want.

*F*rank and Rosemary were talking with their pediatrician. She had just finished her six-month evaluation of their daughter, Alexie. Everything seemed to be fine. Alexie, to quote the doctor, was "right on schedule." The pediatrician asked them to wait a moment while she got some information for them about language development. Frank and Rosemary were confused. Why would the doctor be giving them information about language development? Was the doctor talking about learning to speak another language? Why would they want Alexie to do that? This was rather bizarre. She wasn't even talking in any language now.

How Do Children Develop Language?

MOST INFANTS COME into the world eager, ready, and able to learn language. Their innate capabilities are amazing. They have an inner desire to communicate and the ability to pick up at least the basics with minimal amounts of exposure to language. Of course, as a loving and informed parent, you will want to provide your child with lots of exposure to language so that she can reach her potential as a communicator. But you may be surprised that your child won't need flashcards, lessons, incentives, correction, or bribes to learn language. In fact, such things almost always backfire, boring a child or turning her off to language. Rather, the main tool your child will need to acquire language will be *you*.

> The main tool your child will need to acquire language will be you.

In language learning, consider your child's early years as windows of opportunity. Even before she starts kindergarten, her brain is "wired" to learn a tremendous amount about language and communication. While researchers still debate exactly what that wiring involves—wiring specifically for language learning or a more general wiring for learning a variety of complex systems, including language—you will find your child learns language best when the "wiring" she brought with her into the world encounters your models of language use.

Throughout this book, you will hear us repeatedly say that you should *model* language for your child, not quiz her or make her repeat or imitate you. When we talk about modeling language for your child, we mean that you talk *with* your child, using words and sentences that are related to what she is focused on. It also means that if she says something "incorrectly," you should say what she said, or something similar, the correct way, without asking her to imitate you. Asking your child to imitate you does not allow her to learn *why* she might be saying that particular sound, word, or sentence, or *when* she should say it. Keep this in mind: *Language is developed, not taught.*

Rich language will come out of the ordinary things you and your child do. You don't need lesson plans and she doesn't require elaborate activities and toys. Let her safely explore her environment and the familiar items around her. Encourage imaginative games and symbolic play, and follow up on her natural curiosity. In simple and attentive ways, you can raise an enthusiastic communicator with an interest in the world and lots of interesting things to say.

Do Children Develop Language Similarly?

MOST CHILDREN FOLLOW a similar path of language development. As language development specialists, we have certain milestones for language skills during certain periods or stages (see the chart after the table of contents). However, we also know there is some give and take as far as when certain skills should appear. For example, if your niece uses short sentences at 16 months and your son is still using single words at 20 months, you may be concerned. Yet, we would consider both children to be within the expected range of typical language development. The variability can be affected by children's styles, temperaments, and personalities as they acquire language. Thus, while there is a similar path of language development that most children take, we must acknowledge the flexibility necessary in this area of human development.

As we discuss how children acquire language over the first six years, we also are aware of other factors independent of the child that may affect development. One factor that may affect what a child learns and when she learns it is the family's own cultural and language background. Different cultural groups have different language rules that need to be learned. Some cultural groups may vary in their expectations of what's usual and acceptable for children and parents. One family may expect a three-year-old to be an active participant in conversations and show a strong interest in books, while another family may feel that children should be listeners more than talkers. In chapter 6, we provide some information on cultural styles and differences that may influence language development.

For our review on language development (chapters 1 to 4), we will discuss language acquisition, in a general sense, for children who come from families who represent "mainstream" America. However, we do this for convenience, knowing that modifications in language development due to cultural or language backgrounds that differ from "mainstream" America are equally valid. In other words, children from these cultures learn language in a different way, not a wrong way.

Getting Started

DURING YOUR CHILD'S first six years, you have a great opportunity to help him acquire the most important skill he'll ever learn—the ability to use language. Language is the main way your child will communicate. It involves the sounds and meanings of the words your child uses, how he orders those words into understandable sentences, and how he selects what he says depending on his purpose for communicating. Language is so vital because it's his primary connection to you and others, his path into family and cultural life, his way of expressing himself, and his means of getting his needs met.

Developing language is a complex, fascinating process, one in which you and your child each have essential, intertwining roles. As your child grows, you'll marvel at the ease with which he learns to communicate—so much seems to come naturally.

Yet, you'll also discover that he will benefit in reaching his potential through your active partnership. The whole process is challenging, enjoyable, and rewarding, and one of your best chances to have a positive and lasting effect on your child's life.

As language specialists and parents ourselves, we're intrigued by the process of learning language; we know the joys firsthand, and we also know the uncertainties involved. In the course of our work, we've talked to thousands of parents about their issues and questions. "Why isn't my daughter talking yet?" "I'm so exhausted at night I can't read aloud as much as I think I should." "Is a bilingual sitter okay?" "My older son learned colors and letters a lot faster than my younger one." "Can computers teach my daughter to read?"

We've written this book to give you the information you need, share exciting discoveries in our field, reassure you, and help you succeed with this most important job. You're exposed to a lot of advice from the media and other sources, and we'll help you understand and evaluate what you hear. In chapters 1 to 9, we show you what to expect during your child's first six years and offer practical suggestions for everything from choosing books to maximizing household chores for learning.

How Should I Use This Book?

THERE ARE SEVERAL points we hope you keep in mind as you read this book. Some of these points have to do with how you compare your child to the information you read. Other points deal with how we have chosen to write this book.

Your Child's Language Development

Remember, the main purpose of this book is to help you become a knowledgeable parent on the topic of child language development. This knowledge will serve you well in several situations. First, with your new knowledge in hand, you should be able to resist other individuals or the media who encourage you to push your child and his language skills ahead by sending him to an "academic" preschool or by using flashcards, workbooks, computer programs, or language-oriented videos to *teach* him language. Media sources and businesses promote the notion that children who talk early, know the greatest number of concepts, and read first are the only ones headed for success. These messages help create the pressure many parents feel to give their child some sort of language boost or preschool competitive edge. This advice may be well intentioned, and some of the products may not be "bad" when used as extra experiences for your child. However, such products often treat language as a subject to be taught or drilled, rather than something to be acquired through rich, everyday experiences. The real boosts and edges to enriching your child's language development come from common, everyday, personal interactions between a child and the people who care about him.

A second reason for arming yourself with an understanding of child language development is that you will know how to resist feelings of guilt and shame when you hear well-meaning others report how their child is using a certain language skill way before your child is ("My Johnny can recite the alphabet and count to 100!"). In other words, you will know the range of typical development and feel comfortable whether your child is advanced or just where he should be in development.

Finally, knowing how language typically develops will help you ignore potentially misleading reassurances that come from people who seem to take an overly casual approach to language development and downplay the possibility of problems

("Albert Einstein didn't talk until he was three!"). Should you read the first eight chapters of this book and question your child's language skills, we provide information in chapter 9 that will help you decide what to do, whom to see, and what to say. Be assured that your actions do make a difference to your child's language acquisition, and that it's good to look for help when you suspect a problem. Early intervention can make a world of positive difference to your child.

> The real boosts and edges to enriching your child's language development come from common, everyday, personal interactions between a child and the people who care about him.

The Style of This Book

Although we are child language specialists, as parents we wanted to write this book in an understandable, illustrative way. We believe you should know as much about language development as possible. We also know that your learning should be easy, fun, and engaging. Thus, we have written this book with a few points in mind.

First, because each of us has one son and one daughter, we wanted to give equal time to both genders. So, as you read, you will notice that we alternate between male and female pronouns. In this way, we demonstrate that language development is similar for both boys and girls. Plus, this approach helps us to deal with one of the tricky aspects of English grammar: There is no gender-neutral, singular pronoun! We can say "they" to refer to both boys and girls; however, it means more than one. What do you do when you want to refer to only one person in a general sense? English makes us commit to either a girl (she/her) or a boy (he/him)! We tell you this partly to explain our use of pronouns in this book, but also to begin to give you an appreciation for just how complicated our language system can be! Yet, most children will master the fundamentals somewhat effort-lessly. We can almost guarantee that after reading this book and finding out what language acquisition involves, you will truly be amazed and quite impressed with your child!

Second, although child language specialists and researchers often break language development into a number of small stages or phases, we broke the process down into four main stages, represented by the first four chapters. In each of these

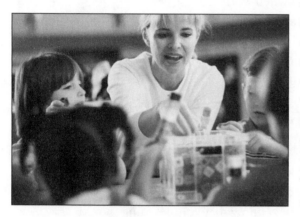

stages, we will use a dif-ferent term for your child, to distinguish that stage of life from the other ones. In chapter 1, we cover your *infant's* first year and the skills she is developing to pre-pare her for her first words. In chapter 2, we discuss your *baby's* first words, which occur dur-

ing the second year of her life. It might seem odd to have a whole chapter about babies who are using only one word at a time. However, this is a critical period of development for chil-dren and one that depicts the complex skill of language in many ways.

Our goal in chapter 3 is to provide you with a wealth of in-formation about your *toddler's* movement from one-word sen-tences to multi-word sentences. This covers your toddler's third and fourth years of life, roughly ending on his fourth birthday. Finally, in chapter 4, we discuss the fifth and sixth years of your *preschooler's* life, when he is not only completing the major developmental portion of learning about spoken language, but also learning the foundation skills for written language (reading and writing).

We also hope that our abundant use of examples, taken from our own children, will shed additional light and understanding on what we discuss. Our children are nearing or in their teen years. However, through their examples over the years, they have helped us better understand and explain to others how children develop language.

Our children are our delights, and we think you will laugh and enjoy them along with us as we provide examples of what they have said or done over the years. Caleb and Caitlin, currently 16 and 12 years old respectively, are the son and daughter of Julie. Nick and Genevieve, 17 and 14 years old, are Kenn's children. To help cut down on unnecessary words, we introduce you to them now. We think you will become quite well acquainted with them as you read through the next four chapters.

Summary

LANGUAGE IS A rich, complex, adaptable system—it's the way we combine sounds, words, signs, and sentences to communicate our thoughts and understand others. Language is how we, as humans, socialize and learn. If, as a parent, you also take this broad and more complete understanding of language, you'll be more likely to look appreciatively and realistically at *all* the dimensions of your child's language development: what he has to say, how he says it, and how he uses language to interact with you and others.

The first six years are indeed exciting. During your child's first six years, she'll acquire the foundation for a lifetime of communication. As she grows, language will continue to be central to most things she does. The stronger her language skills, the better she will be able to express her feelings and explain her ideas and thoughts; connect with family, friends, caregivers, and teachers; pursue her interests and talents; learn both in and outside of school; speak up for herself and watch out for her interests; help and encourage others; gather information so she can make good decisions and evaluate what she hears and reads; and understand new technologies and the changing world. As you can see, language is the bridge to almost any aspect of your child's life. That's why we think it is so important for you to understand how it develops.

We hope you will enjoy this review on how language develops across your child's first six years of life as much as we like talking about it. Language development has become a lifetime study for us, not only because it is our job, but also because we are parents. Like you, we were overjoyed with our children's first *goo*, ecstatic with their first words, mesmerized by their first stories, and surprised with their first written spellings of their names. Join us in this fascinating journey of language development.

Beyond
Baby Talk

Getting Started:
How You and Your
Infant Create
Language Together

DID YOU KNOW?

• At birth, infants prefer their mothers' voices to other women's voices.

• To an infant, the human face is a fascinating object.

• Infants can express many desires and wants before they can talk.

*A*s *young, first-time parents, Jim and Karen were relatively calm and self-assured in their parenting skills for their infant daughter. Three weeks after their daughter's birth, Karen and the baby had a nursing schedule set, and Jim was fast becoming an expert diapering service. They marveled over how beautiful their daughter was and wondered what her voice would be like when she began to talk. They knew children did not talk until about age one, and they were anxious to begin communicating with their little one. However, during that third week, something interesting* *happened. As Jim was changing her diapers, she smiled. He also noticed that her eyes seemed to brighten when Karen spoke from the other room. Suddenly, he realized that his little girl was actually communicating already!*

Believe it or not, this first year of life will contain one of the greatest accomplishments of your infant's life. It is during this first year that she will catch on to the notion of communicating. She will learn to take control of her mouth, forming the sounds of language that will serve her well as she begins to talk. She will learn to relate her needs in more predictable ways that can be easily understood by you. She will develop, in essence, the foundation for all future language learning. And your part in this learning is vital. As you will see, your actions and interactions with her will help her "catch on" to this incredible communication tool: language.

> This first year of life will contain one of the greatest accomplishments of your infant's life.

What Is Language?

THE QUALITY OF your child's life is dependent, to a great extent, on her ability to communicate. Language permeates all aspects of her experience; it's an essential part of her being, how she connects with others, expresses herself, and gets the care she needs. Language is also important because it's your window into your child's personality—her words let you in on her thoughts and feelings. Through language, you are able to guide and influence your child and pass your values on to her.

So, what *is* language? Language is made of five systems or aspects of communication, all equally important, all different from one another. These systems include sound, meaning, word order, grammar, and the social uses of language. Taken as a whole, they represent the rules we must follow when we communicate so that others will understand us and make sense of what we are saying.

The Sound System: Phonology

The first system deals with the speech sounds that we all use when we speak. This aspect of language is formally called phonology. When we speak, we use certain sounds that are accepted by our listeners as valid sounds for communicating. So, for example, we use speech sounds such as *p*, *d*, *k*, *s*, *sh*, and *n*. These speech sounds are the building blocks for exchanging information among individuals. There are other sounds we could make, but if they are not part of the meaningful words that we use to convey meaning, then they are not speech sounds.

Some speech sounds we make are not speech sounds in other languages, and some other languages use sounds that are not speech sounds in our language. For example, Spanish has a trilled *r* sound, whereas English does not. Further, differences that are important in one language may not be important in another. For instance,

The quality of your child's life is dependent, to a great extent, on her ability to communicate.

the difference between the vowel sounds in *seat* and *sit* is important in English. Changing from one to another can result in different words (*beat/bit; seen/sin; leap/lip*). However, this difference is not important in Spanish, which is one of the reasons why native Spanish speakers struggle with those sounds in English and pronounce some of the *i* words with an *ee* sound (*feet* for *fit*). Children acquiring the sound system of their language must learn which sound differences are important (and worthy of attention) and which ones are not (and can be ignored).

It's important here that you understand that we are talking about sounds, not letters. For adults, this is sometimes confusing, because we are so used to thinking about words as made up of letters. The danger to thinking of speech sounds as letters is that sometimes speech sounds are represented by two letters. We write the word *bath* using four letters, but when we say bath, we hear only three speech sounds—*b, a, th*. On the other hand, the letter *x* is just one letter, but when it is said in a word, it represents two sounds—*k* and *s*, as in *box* (*b-o-k-s*).

Thus, when we are talking about children's developing language skills, we are including in that discussion how they learn to articulate or pronounce the sounds that make up their language. As you will see, children must come to understand that certain rules must be followed when speaking. These rules involve including all speech sounds that should be in a word and

using them in the right places of the word, and not adding or using speech sounds that should not be in a word.

Of course, not everyone will use speech sounds when communicating, or using language. Some individuals will use sign language to convey their thoughts and ideas. In this case, then, the aspect of language that involves speech sounds is replaced by the system of hand gestures, movements, and placement around the body. This gestural system is equivalent and as important to communicating through sign language as sounds are for spoken language. The speech sound system is the only component of language that is not shared between spoken language and sign language. The remaining systems are found in both types of language.

The Meaning System: Semantics

Children learn very early in development that they can use words to express lots of different ideas and concepts that they have to offer. As you will see in chapter 2, when your child first learns to talk, he will use several types of words. These words will allow him to discuss actions, request help, comment on passing objects or people, and greet you as you come in the door. He will do this with a set of words that, although limited at first, expands dramatically over the first five years. Thus, semantics involves both general *types* of words and the *meanings* of individual words.

Many people, including some educators, pediatricians, and caregivers, seem to think of early language as though it were synonymous with semantics, the meaning system of language. Often, it seems people talk about language as lists of concepts like colors and numbers; the more concepts a child knows, the better and more advanced his language is. However, as this first section suggests, language involves vocabulary and concepts, and whole lot more.

The Systems for Word Order and Grammar: Syntax and Morphology

Some of you may recall learning Spanish, remembering how confusing it was at first that the order of words was different for English than it was for Spanish. We might say, "I see a red car" in English, but in Spanish, we would say, "Yo veo el coache rojo" (I see car red).

Word order is different for each language. Within each language, we need to follow the rules for which words go where in spoken, and written, sentences. It would not do to talk to others in English using Spanish word order. Imagine the confused looks on others' faces if we started using sentences like, "Liked I my present." We'd sound a lot like Yoda, from the *Star Wars* movies! The system that provides the rules for word order, syntax, is highly structured and rigid. As your child develops language, she will need to learn the rules for how to order her words and what word orderings are allowable. It is quite the task considering no one actually will sit down and tell her which words to put where in a sentence.

Besides word order, we also need to think about the endings and beginnings we attach to basic words and the "filler" words that help us link thoughts across sentences. The term *grammar* (or as we call it, *morphology*) is often used when describing the aspect of the language system that dictates how we let others know about the number of objects we are discussing (two cat*s*), whether we are talking about events in the past, present, or future (I jump*ed* over the fence.), the direction of a moving object (The dog ran *in* the house.), and how to make the subject of the sentence "agree" with the action of the sentence (She *sings*. They *sing*.). The grammar of a language is complex, containing many dos and don'ts. It is not uncommon to hear someone refer to "proper grammar" or comment that an individual's sentence was "grammatically incorrect." While as an adult you may take grammar for granted, we think you will be amazed when you read how children learn this rule system with remarkable ease and speed.

> While as an adult you may take grammar for granted, we think you will be amazed when you read how children learn this rule system with remarkable ease and speed.

The System of Social Language: Pragmatics

Language does not exist in a vacuum. It would make no sense for an individual to have perfect knowledge of the sound, meaning, word order, and grammar systems of a language if that person never used that knowledge to communicate with other human beings. Thus, a very important system of language, pragmatics, or how we use language to socialize, must be learned as well.

In the first five years of his life, your child will learn the many different reasons that humans talk, such as to inform, to question, to warn, and so on. He will learn that he needs to follow specific social rules when talking with others, such as taking turns in conversations, making eye contact with the other person, and revising what he has said when his listener is confused. He also will develop the ability to change the way he talks, depending on who he's talking to. He will talk "politely" to his grandparents and talk "babyish" to his younger sister. When children demonstrate these skills, plus many more, it attests to the fact that they have learned the rules for how we socialize and interact with others using language.

Your infant has been learning since before he was born.

In this chapter, we will cover the language and communication skills your infant is learning during the first 12 months of life. We also will cover the types of interactions parents should use with their infants to help them develop their ability to communicate with others. We find this first year to be completely fascinating. Your infant is starting to crack the code to a skill that is the most important skill he will learn. Let's begin!

The First Six Months of Life

IN THE FIRST few weeks of life, your infant will cry, fuss, cough, hiccup, stare, and sleep. It may seem like he is not learning anything about you or his surroundings. However, he is way ahead of you. He actually has been learning since before he was born.

Listening Skills

Your infant may have already learned to recognize your voice while in the womb. Researchers have found that infants as young as three days old can recognize their mothers' voices compared to other women's voices. While infants have heard their mothers' voices since birth, it seems equally likely that they have been listening to their mothers' voices while still in the womb. Infants also prefer to hear human voices over non-human sounds, although one of our children sure liked the sound of a vacuum cleaner when he was an infant. A parent's voice most often soothes an infant when other devices, such as mobiles and music boxes, just won't do the trick. This is probably not new information to recent parents, who realize that often the only way to soothe their infant is by talking to him with a gentle voice.

An infant's ability to recognize a parent's voice is not the only hearing skill he has at birth. Your infant has come into the world ready to hear differences between the sounds we use for speech. Researchers have studied infants' abilities to hear slight differences between simple speech sounds, such as sounds like *ba* and *pa*. Pairs of speech sounds like *pa* and *ba* were chosen because they are highly similar in the way they sound. They vary only by minor differences in the sound spectrum. To study infants' early listening skills, researchers use specially designed pacifiers and noisemakers that create a sound, such as *pa*. As an infant sucks on the pacifier, the speech sound noises start. Initially, the infant sucks the pacifier repeatedly, enjoying the ongoing sounds of repeated *pa . . . pa . . . pa*. Soon, however, the infant stops sucking because the repetition of the sounds becomes boring. The researchers then switch to a new sound, in this case, *ba*, and the infant starts vigorously sucking again, suggesting that the infant has recognized a difference between the sounds.

> Talk with your infant from his first day of life.

Infants do not do this when researchers use speech sounds that represent different "variations" of the way one particular speech sound can be said (*pa . . . paaaa . . . PA*).

Now, keep in mind that when infants hear differences between sounds, it does not mean they understand that the sounds are meaningful or even part of their parents' language. For example, English-speaking infants will notice differences in speech sounds that are not part of the English language. They also do not hear differences between every pair of sounds, especially if the sounds are similar. In addition, infants are not the only little ones that have these skills. Research has shown us that some other mammals have similar listening skills. These studies tell us that your infant is ready to listen to some of the fine differences in your speech from the moment he is born. As he grows and develops, these listening skills will become stronger, at least for the speech sounds of the language his parents and those around him use. If nothing else, this helps prepare him to be ready to take in all the wonderful language you use when you cuddle him.

So, what do these listening skills and preferences tell us about what parents should do with their newborns? Talk with your infant from his first day of life. He is listening to the fine details of your voice, a voice he prefers over other sounds. And he is learning!

Vocal Skills

Initially your infant's vocal skills will consist primarily of cries and burps, and maybe some *oooooo* type sounds. The sounds she makes will not contain "real" consonants or vowels, at least not like the ones we use. However, soon she will start making noises that seem *almost* like the sounds you make. Within three to four months after birth, your infant will start making vowel sounds and then those *coos* and *goos* that every parent awaits. At first, these *coos* may be almost accidental. When infants are on their back, their tongue naturally lies back against the soft part of the roof of their mouth. This is exactly where we, as adults, make our *ka* and *ga* sounds. As infants begin to make sounds, suddenly a *k* or *g* sound emerges and the result is a sound that is highly similar to *coo* or *goo*. Soon, the infant learns that he can do this willfully, and to the joy of every parent, the infant is *coo*ing and *goo*ing at all times of the day and night, especially in reaction to delightful sights, such as her parents.

Toward the end of the first six months, your infant will broaden her repertoire of sounds. Infants between four and six months often begin to experiment more with their mouth, tongue, and throat. They make raspberry sounds or screeches that sound like the cat out in the alley. These wild sounds and cries are your infant's way of testing her abilities. She is playing with her vocal system and seeing what it can do. Along the way, she also begins to say other new consonant sounds. She may begin to use a *t* or *p* along with a vowel. With practice and better control of her mouth, the number of different sounds she makes and the frequency with which she makes them should increase.

One thing you can do as a parent is react to these sounds your infant is making. When she makes these sounds, go ahead and make them back. In fact, you will probably find yourself interpreting her vocal play as real words (more on that in chapter 2). "Listen" to this particular interchange between Genevieve and her dad when she was nine months old and he was changing her diapers:

Genevieve: "Ahhhhh . . ."

Dad: "Ahhhh. You like that infant powder, don't you? Ooohh, ahhhh."

Genevieve: "Eeeeahhh!"

Dad: "Eeeeahhh? Oh? You are excited about this bath coming up. You love bath time, don't you?"

Genevieve: "Ooooo, Ooooo."

Dad: "Ooooo, oooohhh. That's nice, isn't it?"

This small interchange between parent and child seems almost like a true conversation is occurring. To some extent, this is exactly what is happening, even though the infant is not aware. This is great! "Conversations" such as these will show your infant that you are interested in her and what she has to say. At times, it likely will increase the amount she vocalizes. Pretty soon, the two of you may be having a whole "vocal" conversation!

Interaction Skills

Is your infant ready to interact with you during his first few months of life? Yes, although like his *coo*ing and *goo*ing, it may be somewhat accidental at first. Infants are born with certain abilities and preferences that indirectly lead to wonderful interactions between them and their caregivers. For example, during the first few months after birth, infants prefer to look at objects that are varied in their shapes and lighting. Infants like to see something that has angles and curves, as well as differences or contrasts in lightness and darkness. Perhaps you have seen toy mobiles on the market that are made up of different white and black shapes. These have been developed precisely for this reason. The idea is that infants love to look up at these devices. The exciting thing about this is that you have all the makings for an equally fascinating toy, and it's as clear as the nose on your face. In fact, it is the *nose on your face* . . . and your cheeks, your chin, and your ears. When you hold your infant and he is looking into your face, he is seeing different angles and shadows because of the way the light hits your face. And you didn't pay a thing for this tool!

Speaking of holding your infant so that he is looking at your face, this is an excellent position for your infant, given his visual skills at this time. At first, infants can best focus on objects that are within about eight inches of their face. Think about it. Most parents hold their infant close to their face. Parents want to see their infant and almost intuitively understand their infant wants to see his parent's face, even if at the time it is because of the angle of a chin or the shadowing by a nose. When parents hold their infant this way, they are positioning the infant to take full advantage of his visual range.

Infants also start smiling soon after birth. At first, it may be a nonsocial smile. In other words, your infant may be reacting to internal functions, if you get our drift. However, by about three weeks or so, infants begin to smile in reaction to sights that intrigue them. Again, it might be that a parent's face is particularly interesting because of the angles and shadows. It also might be that the infant is happy to hear a voice that he recognizes. Whatever the reason, the infant smiles and the parents light up.

So, why are we talking about an infant's preference for your face and your voice, and how do these fit under interaction skills? It is because of the *effect* these preferences have on a parent. When you see your infant smile at you, or become seemingly entrenched in staring at your face, or turn when she hears your voice, you will become excited because it seems your infant is interested in *you*. (You may even jump up and, paraphrasing the award-winning actress Sally Field, say: "She likes me, she really likes me!") And then you will enter the "dance" that occurs between parent and infant, that interplay of actions and reactions that will show your infant the importance of what she just did. You will try to get her to listen and look more. You will increase the amount you talk with her. You will be showing her the importance of face-to-face interactions and the exchange of smiles, sounds, and looks. These lessons will serve her well as she begins to learn about language and communicating.

Another significant skill your infant is developing, one that will help prepare her for language learning, is called *joint attention*. Joint attention is when two or more individuals are focused on, or observing, the same object, person, or event. This skill is important for your infant because when the two of you are looking at the same object, your comments about that object have more meaning for her. In other words, she will benefit more from your language models because the language you are using is directly tied to the object of her focus.

Your baby's joint attention skills develop in a systematic way over the first year. During the first few months, she will move through a series of steps in developing this skill. First, she will have the ability to focus on objects placed in front of her face. Next, she will be able to follow objects moved by you, quickly followed by reacting to the language you use that is directed to her. By about four to six months, your baby will be able to follow the direction your eyes take when looking from her to an object. She also will be responding to your directive to "look."

The Second Six Months of Life

YOUR INFANT IS getting older now, and the foundational skills for speech and language are increasing. During this next six months, he will become purposeful in his interactions with you. By the end of this period, and maybe just before, he will say his first word.

> By the end of this period, and maybe just before, he will say his first word.

Vocal Skills

Your infant has been *coo*ing and *goo*ing for some time. He has been using some other sounds, such as squealing and growling. Now he is ready to start babbling.

For most of us, when we think about babbling, we think of an infant saying *goo-goo-gaa-gaa*. In reality, your infant may already have been doing this when he was in that *coo* and *goo* stage mentioned earlier. However, around six months, your infant will begin saying a series of consonants and vowels, or strings of sounds, that reflect the ever growing maturity (control) of his vocal system (his mouth, tongue, throat, and so on). These babbles will contain replications of sounds that typically contain the same series of consonants and vowels. Chances are, the consonant sounds you hear will be such sounds as *p, b, t, d, m, n*, or *w*, because these sounds appear easiest to make in infants' little mouths. Thus, you may hear your infant say such profound statements as: *awawawawawawa, ininininininini*, or *dadadadadada*. Of course, when dad hears the latter string of sounds, he will become very excited because his infant is saying his name. Unfortunately, at this point, there is a slim chance this is actually happening. Again, the infant is experimenting with his newly developing skills. Through these experimentations, he is learning how to make certain sounds and how to sequence sounds together. These are definitely skills that will aid him when he begins to use sounds for real words.

Toward the latter part of these six months, your infant will become even more sophisticated with her babbling. By about eight or nine months, she may start adding variety to her babbles. Now, she will have long strings of sounds that contain several consonants and vowels, such as: *badutigah* or *manmeba*. Along with these, your infant may try to imitate a word that you say, even though she has no clue what it means. She also may imitate the up and down contours of speech, just like those you use when you ask questions or make comments. For example, you infant may produce a whole string of sounds that resemble a long question: *abadudatadutah?* Researchers call this jargon, because it sounds "adultlike" in the *way* it is said, yet it has no meaning. Even if your infant has no idea why she is making these sounds in this way, she is still learning the various ways we use our speech when we talk.

Across these many months, your infant has learned a great deal about his vocal system and its potentials. All of this accidental and purposeful practice has led him to develop a whole repertoire of sounds and combinations of sounds. As he nears his first birthday, you will find that the sounds he uses are much like the sounds you use for real words. You also may find that he seems to have certain sounds or sound combinations he likes because these fill many of his babbling moments. He may even have a sound or series of sounds that seem to act like a word. These "pretend words" are not really words at all. Your infant is not trying to say a word that you always say. Instead, he has made up this particular sound or sound string to stand for a reason to communicate. For example, when Genevieve was about 11 months, she often would say *ga* when she wanted something: her doll, her blanket, her mom, her bottle. This "pretend word" then was her own creation that stood for "I want." Remember, encourage these and any type of babbling and jargon by babbling back and talking to your infant. Pretend you are holding a conversation with him. You are showing him the importance of human interaction.

Interaction Skills

Even though your infant has been crying and *coo*ing and making other noises, she hasn't been purposefully trying to communicate with you up until now. Rather, she has been reacting to the way her body feels or to her environment. When her stomach felt hungry or her bottom was wet, she cried. When she saw an interesting face or pleasing object, she smiled and *coo*ed. However, she was not trying to express her feelings or comment on her environment on her own. Researchers who study infants say that at about eight or nine months, infants begin to intentionally communicate with others to reach a particular goal or objective. In fact, infants will start communicating with their parents, and others, for two main reasons: to comment on what is in their environment and to request an object, action, or person.

At nine months of age, infants do not have words yet, so they try to communicate using other interesting and creative ways, by using gestures and the sounds with which they have been playing. For example, an infant may point at the cow outside her car window and let out an *eeeeeee*, as if to say: "There's a cow out there!" Another time, the infant may reach up with her arms toward her father and let out a grunt, as if to say: "Pick me up, Daddy!" With both of these purposeful actions, the infant's intent to communicate is clear. She wants to let her mother know she sees a cow or to convey that her father should pick her up. When an infant begins to show intentional communication, she has tackled a very important and crucial aspect of language: She is using some recognizable skill to let you know she wants you to listen to her and understand what she is thinking. This skill represents the very reason for communicating: sharing your thoughts and feelings with others.

During the second six months, your baby is taking on more responsibility for establishing and maintaining joint attention. Around six or seven months, she is reaching for objects, which often causes you to focus on that same object. Invariably, you will find that you start talking about that object. Finally, at around eight months of age, your baby will be reaching for toys or other objects, while also looking at you. Often this type of joint attention is saying, "Look, will you help me get this?" As your baby matures, she increases her ability to shift her eye gaze from you to the object and back. This type of "eye signaling" encourages a "dialogue" between the two of you. She looks at you, and then the object, and then back to you. You begin talking about the object, following the lead she has set. She is actually telling you, without words, what the topic of conversation should be. What a powerful skill your baby has developed!

Helping Your Infant Create Language

YOUR INFANT HAS started an incredible journey during this first year of life, one that develops a skill that will affect his whole life. Without language, your child will not be able to express his feelings to others, participate in school or social events with his friends, or interview for a job. That sounds somewhat daunting, doesn't it? Relax, though, because both you and your child bring a lot of tools to help the process as it develops. Your biggest role during this year will be to be a caring, loving parent who recognizes the subtle changes in your child's abilities and reacts and encourages them. This can be done in any situation in which you and your child interact. Below we have listed three common situations—changing time, bath time, and eating time—because we know that these situations occur frequently throughout the day with infants. The suggestions we provide are not unique to any one of these particular situations. Rather, you can use these strategies within any situation.

Changing Time

As a parent of an infant, you undoubtedly are finding yourself changing your little one *multiple* times a day. Let's focus on changing clothes, even though you likely are changing his diapers more often! Are there specific things you can do and say during this time that will facilitate your infant's developing communication skills? Of course!

Not unlike your own clothes-changing routine (first the right leg, then the left leg), you probably have already established certain routines as you change your infant's clothes (first the right arm, then the left arm). Along with these specific, routine acts, you may find yourself saying the same thing: "Okay, first we take out this arm. Then we take out that arm. Ooooh. Naked baby! Naked baby!" At first, your infant hears a long string of sounds, without any specific awareness of where words stop and start. Perhaps it sounds like this: "Okfirstwetakeoutthis arm. Thenwetakeoutthatarm. Ooooh. Nakedbaby! Nakedbaby!" However, as he hears the same types of language (not identical, but similar) accompanying the same actions, he will begin to identify which word or words go with which objects or actions. Thus, unlike other situations where routine leads to quick boredom on your part, routines such as these are actually excellent learning experiences for your infant. Don't hesitate, then, to use routines for valuable language-learning experiences. During these everyday happenings, talk to your infant using similar types of words and sentences.

> As you change your infant's clothes, he may very well start to oooh and ahhh. Take advantage of these vocailzations by ooohing and ahhhing back.

As you change your infant's clothes, you most likely will be in close proximity to him (well, except for those really nasty diapers). Remember, this is exactly where you want to be. You are providing your child with the "scenery" he truly enjoys. As your child enjoys the shapes and shadows of your face, he may very well start to *oooh* and *ahhh*. Take advantage of these vocalizations by *oooh*ing and *ahhh*ing back to him. Give meaning to his *ooohs* and *ahhhs*, so that he begins to see what he "says" is valuable and meaningful to you.

Bath Time

Just as with changing time, you most likely will fall into certain routines or actions that repeat across bathing times. Talk about what you are doing each time, just like you did during changing time. Remember, you are helping your child begin to identify the words that belong to the objects and actions for that routine. This is true for your infant whether he is four months old or 11 months old.

You also can encourage your infant's joint attention skills during bath time. Most infants beyond two months of age enjoy watching you repeatedly pour water out of the cup into the bath or bob the little yellow ducky under the water and back out. You can use these actions to help develop your baby's ability to change focus from you to the object (falling water or bobbing ducky) and back again, encouraging and establishing joint attention with your little one.

Mealtime

Early on, whether your baby is breast-fed or bottle-fed, you will be holding your child within the physical proximity that best matches her visual range. Thus, during these times, you can focus on your child's face, talking to her as she eats. This models for her good eye contact and encourages face-to-face interactions.

When your baby moves beyond these types of feeding to other kinds of food, you then can take advantage of her growing joint attention skills to talk about what you are doing and the objects involved. The point here is not to try and teach your child by simply labeling the objects and actions, such as: "This is a spoon. These are peaches. I'm feeding you." Not only would that sound silly, it would not be a

> During mealtime, you can focus on your child's face, talking to her as she eats.

particularly helpful language-learning experience. Rather, you can simply talk about what is happening as it happens: "Okay, let's get the spoon. Here are some peaches. Scoop some up.

Yummy, yummy peaches." In this way, you are providing names or labels for the actions in which you are involved, providing lots of opportunities for your infant to start recognizing what objects and actions are called in her world.

Chapter Summary

MANY PEOPLE WOULD not assume that infants are developing language in their first year of life. When there are no words, how can you say children have language? As you have read in this chapter, children are learning a lot, and proving it, in their first year of life.

Throughout this first year of life, your child will learn a great deal about this system we call language. You are probably the most important variable in that learning process. Between you and your child, all the raw materials needed for language learning are available. Enjoy these first 12 months, and recognize all the important skills he is learning. And be prepared. He's about to say his first word!

2

Earliest Words: Discovering Your Baby's Style

DID YOU KNOW?

- Babies often rely on the sounds in a word when deciding whether to say the word.
- Some babies practice talking just for the sake of it.
- Reading to your baby now is a valuable learning experience for her.

The college student had been assigned to watch the mother and her baby son play together. He was to observe how the mother interacted with her son and how the son reacted. Over the course of a week, he noticed that the mother frequently repeated what her baby boy said. If the boy said, "Ball," then the mother said, "Ball? Oh, you want me to throw the ball?" It seemed to the college student that this mother always repeated or talked about what the boy was saying. That seemed strange! Why not tell the baby new things, like about her day or about the upcoming three-day weekend? Then the college student noticed something. When the young mother talked to her baby this way, the baby looked at her. He seemed to talk more. And in fact, just now, the baby actually used two words together. Hmm? Maybe there was something to this type of talking.

Many parents view the appearance of their baby's first word as one of the most exciting events in their child's development. What will the first word be? What will her voice sound like? All those months of diapering and sleep deprivation seem to be worth it when that child looks at you and says your name. In this chapter we'll talk about the many factors that lead to and influence how and why your baby says a word. We will review how you can determine that what she says is a real word, why she chooses to say other words besides your name, and what communication strategies you can use to help the language learning process to develop further.

> All those months of diapering and sleep deprivation seem to be worth it when that child looks at you and says your name.

This second year of life is a fascinating one. Your baby is entering into what child language researchers call the one-word stage. Your baby will start off this year with a first word. And as the year comes to a close, she likely will begin combining words into two-word sentences. In between these times, she will be learning new words, words with different meanings and various functions. This is an awesome task for such a young person. You have a definite role in this task. Let's begin.

What Is a Word?

THE ANSWER TO this question might seem obvious; however, identifying a child's first use of a "true" word is a little tricky. As you learned in the last chapter, babies are pretty noisy. They're babbling and making lots of different sounds and maybe some "pretend words" before they actually produce their first true word. In order to identify when a child produces his first word, researchers had to agree on the definition of a word. They came up with four characteristics that we use to qualify a group of speech sounds as a word.

First, we consider the group of speech sounds, that is, the production itself. It should have a clear vowel that sounds close to the actual vowel one expects for that word. Second, it should be a single production followed by a brief period of silence. This is in contrast to babbling, which consists of long strings of consonants and vowels. Third, a true word is used under specific recurring conditions; that is, the word refers to a particular person, thing, or situation. Fourth (and this is our favorite), true words are used in conversations with people! The baby is revealing his budding appreciation of the communicative value of speech and language. Let's look at one example.

> Identifying a child's first use of a "true" word is a little tricky.

Caleb's first word was his own version of our dog's name. His production for *Chi-Chi* sounded somewhat like he was clearing his throat—it had a consonant sound that sounded like a cross between an *h* and a *k*. However, the vowel sounded just like the "long *e*" sound in Chi-Chi's name. Further, his production was consistent, both in terms of the sounds he used and the conditions under which he used it. He produced his version of her name whenever Chi-Chi walked into the room. Finally, he would produce her name and then wait. Sometimes he seemed to be labeling her, other times he seemed to be calling her to come to him. It was a bittersweet moment. He definitely was using her name with purpose. It was just a little sad that his first word referred to the dog rather than his mom.

Most babies use their first true words between 9 and 12 months of age, although there is some variability among babies. The size of their vocabulary increases steadily for the next few months, as they use their one-word "sentences."

What Words Will My Child Use?

CALEB'S FIRST WORD was his dog's name. Why was that the case? All words are not created equally for use by your little one. Your baby's choice of the specific words that will make up her first vocabulary, or set of words that she can say, is influenced by five factors. We consider each of these in the following sections.

Environment

All of our children included the word *computer* in their early vocabulary, but none of them used the word *tractor*. We know

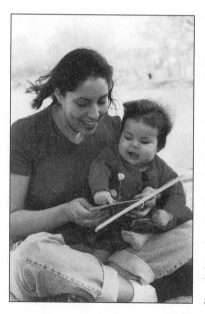

of other children whose early vocabulary was just the opposite; that is, they used *tractor* but not *computer*. As you might guess, the difference in word use is due to the differences in the children's environments, such as their home, their day care, and so on. To a certain extent, children are going to use the words that they hear. Babies who live on a farm are more likely to use words like *chicken* or *tractor* than children who live in the city. Our children heard their parents use the word *computer*, saw their parents using a computer, and even tried using a computer themselves a few times during this early stage of development. Knowing that a baby's first words are influenced by those that she hears may tempt the parent to repeat *mommy* or *daddy* several times during the day in order to increase the chances that she'll use one of those words. Trust us—it doesn't really work! There are other factors that also play a role in the words that make up your baby's first vocabulary.

Word Type

Have you ever considered that a baby might say words such as *run* or *eat* during this one-word stage, but probably won't include words such as *think* or *watch*? This is because the latter words are more abstract, or complex, than the former. Many of the words in a baby's early vocabulary consist of nouns, which are names for people and objects. However, other kinds of words also are used. Simple verbs that refer to common actions, such as *drink* or *go*, are used. Babies also will use social and occurrence words, such as *bye-bye, allgone, another,* and *again* to describe current circumstances. Some children use descriptive words, such as *hot* or *pretty*. Sometimes, to the dismay of the parents, one of the most frequently occurring early words is *no*. It's rare indeed to find a child who isn't quite proficient at using the word *NO!*

These different types of nouns, verbs, and descriptive words form the meaning system of your child's language system. We call this meaning system semantics. Your baby's semantic development is the hallmark of this one-word stage.

Sounds in the Word

Do you remember how difficult it was to say some words when you were a child? Words such as *statistics, aluminum,* and *breakfasts* may come to mind. The word structure, in terms of its speech sounds and number of syllables, can influence whether a baby will attempt to say it during the early stages of language development. In general, words containing several syllables are harder for babies to say than one- or two-syllable words. This is why you're more likely to hear *choo-choo* or *train* than *locomotive*.

Babies' first words can be influenced by the actual sounds that a word contains. Most children produce sounds like *p, b, n,* and *w* before they produce sounds like *g, s, ch, r,* and *l.* This is because the latter are somewhat harder to articulate. Of course, there are individual differences, and some babies may actually produce some of the harder sounds before they do the easier ones.

There is one more interesting point about how speech sounds in words affect what your baby will say first. Many babies may have a preference for certain speech sounds or types of syllables. It is unclear why they seem to prefer certain sounds and sound combinations, but nevertheless, they may capitalize on these preferences when choosing words to add to their vocabulary. Thus, they may choose to say words that match closely their sound preferences and avoid, or choose not to say, words that contain speech sounds and syllables that are quite different than their preferences. The following example, that proved to be somewhat disappointing to the mother involved, illustrates this principle.

> Many babies may have a preference for certain speech sounds or types of syllables.

When Caleb was a baby, he preferred sounds that were made in the middle or back portion of the mouth over sounds made in the front. When he was babbling, we heard a lot more syllables with *t, d, n,* or *k* than with *m* or *b.* This unfortunate preference carried over into his selection of first words, and he produced the word *Daddy* long before he produced the word *Mama*. Years later, when Caitlin was born, her mother was delighted to notice a strong preference for front sounds present in her babbling. The sounds *p* and *b*, which are made on the lips like an *m*, were actually produced more frequently than *t* or *d*, although she said these other speech sounds occasionally. Tragically, however, Caitlin had a strong avoidance of nasal sounds (those sounds made through the nose, like *m* and *n*), and this carried over to her selection of meaningful words. Her poor mother had to once again hear her child saying *Daddy* many times before she ever said *Mama*.

Caitlin's first use of *Mama* was striking, though. Her family had a "night-night" routine that was followed each evening. Her parents would say "night-night" and sing songs, say prayers, and so on. Caitlin would respond several times with "digh-digh," her version of "night-night." One evening she surprised us (and herself) by saying, "Nigh-nigh." Like one of those cartoons that has a light bulb appearing over the head as a concept clears, Caitlin's face brightened up and she said, "Mama!" Of course, we knew better, but it almost seemed like she was thinking, "Nasal sounds! Now I know how to do nasal sounds! I can say *Mama*!"

Usefulness

We've been talking about how characteristics of the words themselves (word meaning or semantic complexity, speech sounds in the word) influence whether a word will appear in your baby's first vocabulary. In addition to these factors, a child's choice of words is also determined by how useful a particular word may be to her. One of the classic examples from past studies of children's language development is that babies typically produce *sock* and *shoe* before they produce *shirt* or *shorts*. This is because babies can manipulate their own socks and shoes before they can do much with their shirts or shorts. Moms and dads are likely to see discarded shoes and socks lying on the floor long before they will see discarded shirts or shorts (a blessed fact that all too soon will change). Thus, babies say the words *shoes* and *socks* early more often than other clothing terms. The degree of usefulness, then, is probably the major reason that the word *no* is used so frequently. It's quite powerful for the child because it can be used in many (all?) situations.

> Babies say the words *shoes* and *socks* early more often than other clothing terms.

Style

SOME PEOPLE ARE born risk-takers. You know the type. They're the ones who can be found bungee jumping, riding dirt bikes, snowboarding, or engaging in other types of extreme experiences. On the other end of the continuum, you find the analytical, cautious person. Once again, you know people like this. They read reviews in trade magazines and do price comparisons for weeks or even months before they actually make a purchase. These same "styles" often characterize babies learning language. On one end of the continuum, we have the cautious calculator. Terms such as referential and noun-lover have been used to describe this style of acquiring language. As these terms suggest, these babies tend to prefer to label people and objects in their environment. They have sound preferences or avoidances that influence the words they will attempt. Later, when they start combining words, their new sentences tend to consist primarily of real words and less "jargon." On the other end of the style continuum, we have our little risk-taker. Terms such as expressive and noun-leaver have been used to describe this style. These babies are about actions and interaction. They have lots to say and they don't seem to feel the need to wait until they can speak clearly before jumping right in to talk! Although they still use a lot of nouns, they are more likely to use other kinds of words *(bye-bye, more, again, no)* quite frequently.

Which style is better for developing language? The answer is *neither*. Both are just fine. Although the noun-lover child might have a slightly larger vocabulary in the earliest stages of development, the differences disappear over time. Interestingly, studies indicate that similarities in style between parents and children can facilitate language. Researchers have found similar styles in mothers as they interact with their babies. When there is a match in style (referential parent-referential baby; expressive baby-expressive parent), language development seems to be slightly enhanced. Finally, it's important to keep in mind that most children don't fall at one of the extreme ends of the style continuum, just as most of us adults fall somewhere between the person who wants to climb Mt. Everest and the person who could write a book on minivans by the time the purchase is done. The point here is that parents should try to match their style of interaction and language to their baby's, *if* there seems to be a strong tendency to one type or the other.

> One of the most powerful ways to influence your child's language use is to model appropriate word use.

Understanding the influences upon the words a baby is likely to use during the single-word stage can be helpful for parents. For one thing, it may make you less anxious if your baby is not using some words even though he has heard them several times and many people in his life want him to use them. Let's face it, *Aunt Mildred* may be one of your son's favorite people, but he might not attempt to say her name because it contains some hard sounds.

Second, knowing what kinds of words may be reasonably expected can help you emphasize those words as you interact with your baby. One of the most powerful ways to influence your child's language use is to model appropriate word use. Modeling is most effective when the language examples are reasonable or feasible for the child. Regardless of how many times we might model the *Preamble to the Constitution* for our baby, chances are he's just not going to recite it back for us! When you really think about it, why would we want him to do that? More than ever, parents feel pressure to make their children into superstars. Get them started in dance, music, sports, foreign languages, reading, and everything else as soon as they are born! When it comes to facilitating language, the best rule is to model words that will be meaningful for your child, words that will help him fit into his environment, words that will help him communicate with the people that he loves! So, think about the five factors that influence a baby's first words and make sure that your child's *environment* consists of multiple models of the right *type* of words that contain *simple sounds*, are maximally *useful,* and fit with her *style* preferences for communicating.

> Researchers have documented babies who can be heard saying words over and over again in their cribs, seemingly just to practice how to pronounce the words.

Social Language Skills

THE ONE-WORD STAGE is characterized by so much more than just the use of one-word sentences. Babies are social beings and thus are interested in using language to socialize. Before they say their first words, babies are socializing in non-language ways, such as through gestures, grunts, and so forth.

Their social language skills, called pragmatics, are beginning to broaden this year. Now babies quite cleverly are using their expanding language skills for a variety of purposes.

As you know, babies use words to label people (*Daddy*) or objects (*kitty*). However, they also use words to request action or information. For example, a baby might point and say *cookie,* not because she's informing you that the little round thing should be called a cookie, but because she wants you to give it to her! Imagine a young baby looking at a book with his dad. He points to a picture of an animal and says, "*Lion?*" In this instance, he is likely requesting information. Other babies have a "one-word version" of the question, "What's that?" It may sound something like *sat* and is said in a questioning manner, often accompanied by pointing. These are two examples of the way in which babies may request information.

Every parent is aware that young children use the word *no* to protest! Protests are not necessarily limited to the word *no.* Children can protest with the word *mine* as someone tries to take a toy away. Babies also use single words to call or greet someone. Some of our fondest memories of our young children were those early mornings when we'd hear our baby calling us from the nursery or when we'd come home and see that excited face as one of our children said *Mom* or *Dad.* Just as we respond to another adult when called or greeted with "Here I am" or "Hi," so we should respond when our babies call or greet us.

Finally, babies sometimes use language simply for practice. The practice function is indeed useful in the early stages of language. Researchers have documented babies who can be heard saying words over and over again in their cribs, seemingly just to practice how to pronounce the words. Sometimes your child may not want or expect a response from you or anyone else in her environment. She may just want to experiment a little with these incredible new skills she is acquiring.

We've discussed the reasons that children use language at the single-word stage. What about topics? What are young babies talking about? Margaret Lahey, one of the pioneers in child language research, writes that early language refers to "what the child is doing, what the child is about to do, or what the child wants others to do." What a great way to capture the focus of a baby's language: Her language use is definitely focused on her world!

We've talked about how powerful modeling is as a tool for facilitating language development in your baby. Knowing that your baby should be using language to label, call, greet, and protest should encourage you to include all of these uses in the language that you model for him. We've seen many parents who are quite adept at modeling the labeling function. This is great, but we hope you'll also remember that calling, greeting, and protesting are also important. At first glance, it may seem a little odd to suggest to a parent that you should help you baby become good at protesting. Many veteran parents will tell you that babies don't need any help in this area! However, in the first stages of language, babies are still learning about the power of words. Given that probably all children are born with the desire to protest, you might as well capitalize on this desire as a way to show the usefulness of language.

Opportunities to model all of these different uses of language occur in everyday, natural activities. There's simply no need to contrive or set up unique "teaching experiences." It's actually best to comment about business as usual each day. Keep in mind, just as your baby's early one-word sentences will be mostly about his world, so should *your* language models be focused on the people, objects, or actions to which your child is attending at the moment. Your baby is focused on the "here and now" of the world. He is not able to talk about and probably not interested in what happened yesterday or what will happen tomorrow. Talk about what he is doing at that moment and you will have an attentive, active language learner.

Child-Directed Speech

YOU'VE PROBABLY NOTICED that you can usually tell when someone is speaking to a child. There's a special way that adults (and, by the way, older children) talk to young children. The interesting thing is that humans seem to do this quite naturally (typically, no one teaches another person to talk like this). Researchers refer to this style of talking (or "register") as child-directed speech (CDS). Initially, this language style was labeled "motherese." However, the term changed to CDS when the style was observed in fathers as well as individuals who weren't even related to the babies with whom they were interacting.

Characteristics of Child-Directed Speech

There are specific features that distinguish CDS from the typical style of speech and language. If you listen to a speaker of CDS, you'll notice a special rhythm and pitch. There is somewhat of a musical quality to CDS. Overall, the pitch is higher. Plus, the speaker's pitch goes up and down more often than during typical speech. CDS speakers also tend to use a slower rate. It is as though they have an unconscious appreciation for the notion that the baby may need a little more time to take in or understand the incoming information.

When using CDS, speakers tend to use simple words. You're likely to hear a word like *choo-choo* or *train* in a conversation with a baby, but you probably won't hear *locomotive*. CDS speakers use shorter sentences. Not only do the sentences contain fewer words, but they also have simple grammar structures. For example, you are more likely to hear, "See the ball? Big ball. Roll ball," rather than, "Look at the rather large ball. Will you roll it to me?" People using CDS will stress, or put more emphasis on, the important words in the sentence. They may simplify the way words are said. For example, some parents may use terms like *blankie* and *ba-ba* for blanket and bottle.

Finally, CDS is characterized by a high degree of responsiveness. Adults using CDS are likely to respond to babies' barely meaningful productions as though they were profound statements. Several years ago, there was a television ad for a long-distance company. Two young parents and their baby were sitting on a floor and a telephone was handed to the baby, who happily produced a string of babbled syllables. It sounded something like "babadigawawikuwu." One of the parents took the phone and said proudly, "Did you hear that, Mom? She said *Grandma!*" Well, perhaps this is a little bit of a stretch; however, it's a great example of being responsive. Your baby will want to repeat activities such as these that make her feel good, successful, and so on.

As a footnote, we should mention that many children and adults use CDS when they talk to animals. Caleb and Caitlin can always tell when their mother is talking to a dog or a cat. Now they do the very same thing. The style of speaking that many people use when talking to animals shares most of the characteristics of CDS.

Effects of Child-Directed Speech

So why do adults talk this way to babies? Researchers have explored the purpose and effects of CDS. They concluded that adults aren't using this register, or language style, in a conscious effort to teach language to babies. If this were the case, it would be very difficult to explain the use of this register with animals. Instead, adults seem to be using it to maximize the chances for optimal communication *and* to express affection. The latter purpose probably explains the use of "animalese" with our pets.

As for the effects, you should know that, in general, using CDS is a very good thing to do! Researchers have found benefits such as greater vocabulary and better grammatical accuracy in babies whose mothers use CDS. With the exception of word simplifications, CDS likely results in more appropriate models. Further, CDS gives the baby confidence to be an active participant in conversations. Features such as attributing meaning to the baby's comments that might not really be so meaningful encourage her to take part in the interaction.

Some people might think that CDS sounds "silly" or "condescending" and shouldn't be used. Nonsense! Enjoy your baby at this level of development. Believe us, it will be over before you know it. On the other hand, the use of CDS is not absolutely crucial for language development. Several studies have shown that children who are not exposed to CDS, or even those who may miss a lot of exposure to typical language models, go on to develop language with a minimum amount of normal linguistic input.

Helping Your Baby Learn to Use Words

YOUR BABY IS taking a giant step in language development this year. He is beginning to use the code that his family has been using around him for over a year. As he begins to express himself with words, you can help that learning along by optimizing your interactions with him. This can occur in all situations, including reading time and playtime.

Reading Time

It is hard to exist in today's world without hearing how important it is to read to your baby. We cannot emphasize enough how true this is. However, what you may not realize is that even at this age, your baby's second year of life, reading is an important activity. By establishing a book-reading routine with your child at this early age, you are helping your child realize early on how important reading is. You also are setting up a routine that will, it is hoped, last far be-yond even when your child can read to himself.

> By establishing a book-reading routine with your child at this early age, you are helping your child realize early on how important reading is.

In this second year of life, reading time with your child may only last five minutes, if that. Don't get frustrated, though. For some babies, this is all the time they choose to devote to this activity, and that's okay. As you hear so many other places, at this point in development, it's the quality, not the quantity, of the time you spend with your child.

The books you choose for your child should be relatively simple. You will find books that allow you to label pictures of objects, people, and actions that are *familiar* to your child will likely be most interesting to him. As you read, talk about the pictures of the objects, pointing to them as you label them. After several readings, you might occasionally ask your child to label the pictures ("Where's the ball?").

Why do we say to only occasionally ask your baby to label pictures? First, as we mentioned in chapter 1, children want their parents to be parents, not teachers. If you begin to turn parent-child interaction times into *quiz times,* you may actually decrease your baby's willingness and desire to interact with you. Similarly, you want to refrain from asking your baby to imitate your naming of pictures. Directed imitation won't help your child know when to use a word or why it is used. However, if you find that your child *chooses* to use a word after you have said it, that's great! Child-initiated imitations, or reproductions of what you have said, show you that your baby is starting to understand that particular word or reason for talking.

Research suggests that children of varying ages tend to choose to imitate another person's language when they are preparing to use that type or level of language themselves. So, when your baby chooses to imitate something you have said, echo back that word and expand on it, or add extra information to it. This might sound like the following:

> Parent: "Look, a truck."
> Baby: "Truck."
> Parent: "Yes, truck. A big truck."

When you respond to your baby this way, you are saying that you understood what he said, that it had meaning, and that he can even add more information later, as he matures. Quite a bit for you to help him learn in such a small amount of time!

Some babies really like to name pictures and objects while other babies don't have this preference.

There is one other reason for why you don't want to ask your baby to label pictures after you have named them. As we said earlier, some babies really like to name pictures and objects while other babies don't have this preference. As we will continue to say, you want to match your language and activities to your baby's preferences the best you can, if he seems to have a fairly strong preference.

Playtime

This year, your baby will be doing plenty of exploring of her environment. As she moves around her little world, she is learning so many new ideas and concepts, such as how certain actions can cause other actions to occur and how objects can disappear and then reappear. She is discovering ways to make some objects or toys represent real objects. As she is learning all this new information, she will likely be talking about it. It is all so new and exciting! However, because of her focus and interests, chances are she won't necessarily want to talk a whole lot about what *you* are doing. This means that playtime should be focused on *her* interests. If she wants to play with the dollhouse and its people, follow this interest and play along with her, commenting on what you, your baby, and the dolls are doing. This child-centered play/focus, rather than a parent-centered play/focus (introducing an activity or toy your baby is not focused on), will most likely result in an increase in her use of words.

Playtime also is the time to follow your baby's language style. As you and your baby play, you may find that she prefers to play games that involve naming, such as the "What's this?" or the "Where's your (body part)?" games. If you see a preference for this, chances are your baby is more of a referential or noun-lover word learner. This doesn't mean she won't learn other words, but it does mean that you can encourage learning by playing the games to which she seems to respond well. Likewise, if your baby seems to enjoy games such as "peek-a-boo" and "this little piggie," the types of games where your child is expected to contribute a whole series of "words" (*peek-a-boo*) or sounds *(wee-wee-wee),* there is a chance she leans more to the expressive or noun-leaver style.

Follow your baby's lead, then. As you play with the dollhouse, encourage the noun-lover baby to use her words by modeling labeling of items as you play, such as: "Look! A dog, a cat, a baby. Lots of things!" The noun-leaver baby can be encouraged to use her words by modeling phrases such as: "Bye-bye Daddy. Car goes vroom-vroom."

The point is that, as we mentioned, we don't want to force babies into styles they don't prefer. Perhaps the best example of this took place between Nick, definitely more of a noun-leaver, and his dad, who really wanted Nick to say *juice* correctly. Nick used the word *dada* to say *juice*, regardless of who happened to have juice or where the juice was. In other words, it was a true word, even though it did not seem to be close at all to the actual adult pronunciation.

Nick (pointing at juice): "Dada."

Dad: "Juice? Say juice."

Nick: "Dada."

Dad (emphasizing the pronunciation more): "Juuuuice."

Nick: "Dada."

Dad (becoming a little impatient and forceful): "Juuuuiiiccee!"

Nick: "Daaaa daaaaa."

This example demonstrates two very important points. First, Nick was not a noun-lover. Even though he was trying to produce a noun, his interest was more in the action of getting it than saying it anywhere near correctly. Second, imitation and demands for accuracy by a parent typically result in an unsuccessful outcome. In this case, however, we can happily report that the dad gave up, never to bring up the issue again (until this book, of course!).

Chapter Summary

WHEN YOU THINK about it, the English language is really complex! When we teach introductory classes on language development, we tell our students that they should leave the class feeling like a genius; that once they find out just how much there is to acquiring a language, they will want to pat themselves on the back for having done it so well! During this second year of your baby's life, he has taken a giant step forward. Using many different strategies and preferences, he has begun to use true words. He has developed the basis for all future language, the ability to communicate with others using the same language system others around him use. And, even though you have provided wonderful language models and created meaningful learning situations, he has done a great deal of the learning on his own, as well. He is now ready to move on to another major milestone, linking words together. The miracle of language development continues!

3

Building First Sentences: Natural Ways to Encourage Your Toddler

DID YOU KNOW?

- The word *no* can mean many different things.
- Toddlers are language inventors.
- Three-year-olds can talk about the past and the future.

*J*ay was driving his three-year-old son, Anthony, home from day care. As usual, Jay was quizzing his son about what had occurred during the day. In the past, Jay would ask a question about one of Anthony's favorite pastimes, like "Did you finger paint today?" Anthony's typical response would be "yeah," possibly followed by a statement like "big boat" or "paint car." Jay loved these conversations, especially because lately he was noticing that Anthony's language skills were improving. It seemed in the last few weeks or so, Jay's responses were more like "Yeah, I paint green *tree" or "I painted me!" Today, Jay asked the familiar question again. However, he wasn't prepared for Anthony's response: "Well, actually . . . painted a yellow house." Jay was shocked. Where did that "actually" come from?*

Your toddler has been producing single words for some time now. It's been amazing to watch her vocabulary steadily increase. Some time around your toddler's second birthday, she'll surprise you by combining two of those words to form her first "sentence." About the same time, her vocabulary will explode, and it will seem like she is learning more new words than you can keep straight! It was certainly that way with our own children. Even as researchers interested in child language development who had plenty of tools available to record our children's every move, we had trouble keeping up with what was happening in our children's language at this stage of development.

By the end of this period, you'll be able to carry on a respectable conversation with your toddler!

In this chapter, we've organized our discussion around developments in the toddler's sound system, vocabulary, types of words, sentences, grammar, and social language skills. We cover the period of language development that begins with the toddler's first two-word combination and ends around the time she is ready for early reading and writing activities (ages four and five). We must warn you—this period has probably received more attention from researchers than any other. That's because so many noticeable changes occur in the toddler's language skills during this time. By the end of this period, you'll be able to carry on a respectable conversation with your toddler! So, fasten your seat belt for an exciting adventure into a toddler's budding use of impressive language structures.

What Kinds of Words Will My Toddler Use?

AS WE SAID earlier, one of the most striking characteristics of this stage is the sheer number of words being added to your toddler's vocabulary on a regular basis. When the first two-word sentence is used, most toddlers have a vocabulary ranging from about 30 to 50 words. By the time the toddler reaches age three, she'll probably be using over one thousand words and understanding even more.

Not only are toddlers rapidly acquiring new words during this period, they also are expanding the *types* of words they use. In the last chapter, we discussed how most early words were labels, simple action verbs, description words, and specific words such as *no, bye-bye,* and *allgone*. During the third stage of development, toddlers will use more and more words that fall within these categories. For example, the descriptive category will increase from simple words such as *pretty* and *hot* to more sophisticated words like *nice, fast,* and *sick*. Additionally, several new *kinds* of words will emerge. Your toddler will use verbs that express an internal feeling or condition, such as *want* and *need*. Later, other verbs that refer to the five senses will be used, including *see, hear, touch, smell,* and *taste*. Even more sophisticated verbs, which represent mental processes, will appear at the end of this stage. Examples include *think, know, wonder,* and *dream*. Verbs aren't the only category that changes. We also see toddlers start using words that refer to number concepts, such as *many, some, two,* and *four,* and time concepts, such as *now* and *then*. In fact, there are so many new words and word types developing during these

> By the time the toddler reaches age three, she'll probably be using over one thousand words and understanding even more.

two years that we could probably fill up the rest of this book with them.

What Kinds of Sentences Will My Toddler Use?

AS WE SAID earlier, the combination of two words into one sentence marks the beginning of a new developmental stage. The ability to combine words helps the toddler gain even more "mileage" out of the words he knows. Instead of saying only "more," he can now be more specific, "more juice" or "more cookie." With word combinations, less confusion about the toddler's intent will occur.

Word Combinations

These early combinations consist of words that the toddler had been using as single-word sentences up to this point. This is an important factor for parents to keep in mind. As we said, your toddler's vocabulary is expanding both in number and type of words that he knows. However, his first sentences will likely consist of those words (and word *types*) that have been around awhile. You heard productions such as *mama, daddy, cracker, more, bye-bye, no, allgone, pretty,* and *go* in the last stage. Now you'll hear these same words in basic sentences, *more cracker, daddy bye-bye, no night-night,* and so on. Toddlers, like adults, can only handle so many new tasks at any one given time. You'll likely hear new words and new word types appearing as single-word sentences initially. Gradually, these new words and word types also will be used in word combinations.

Early Grammar

Not only is your toddler now producing little sentences by combining words, he also is beginning to use English grammar. Grammar means using word endings and smaller words like *is, are,* and *am.* For example, at the beginning of this stage, your toddler might observe the family pet and say, "Doggie bark." After a while, however, he'll say, "Doggie barking." This is so smart! He is showing his appreciation for the notion that the *-ing* ending form tells us something important about the timing of the action, that the action is occurring right then. Language researchers consider the inclusion of grammar forms such as the *-ing* or plural *-s* or past tense *-ed* to be as impressive as adding another whole word to the sentence. The first forms of grammar appear a short time after the toddler starts using word combinations. Gradually, other forms will be added.

> The first forms of grammar appear a short time after the toddler starts using word combinations.

As toddlers attempt to figure out the use of these forms, some interesting language productions result. For example, Caleb once had an action-figure toy that could be seen in the dark. After the first night with the toy, he proudly proclaimed, "My dinosaur glew all night!" He had never heard that form used at home. We promise! When you hear a toddler use a word like that, you recognize it as a mistake—the past tense form for *glow* is *glowed* rather than *glew.* On the other hand, like his mother, you probably can appreciate how clever and creative Caleb was to come up with that word. It makes perfect sense: Today I *blow*; yesterday I *blew.* Today I *grow*; yesterday I *grew.* Why not "Today I glow; yesterday I glew"? Errors such as this one illustrate that language acquisition isn't a "giant memory task." Toddlers aren't memorizing every form they hear for future use. Instead, they are trying to "solve the puzzle," "crack the code," so they will be equipped to create sentences that they haven't heard before. Such creative geniuses are bound to make some mistakes along the way!

Word Order in Sentences

You know that your toddler's first sentences will be somewhat incomplete ("more cookie" for "I want some more cookies"). Gradually, words and other aspects of grammar will fill in the missing gaps. However, the process may seem a little odd to the watchful parent because even though the right words are added to the sentence, they might not be used in the correct order at first. The development of questions and negative forms *(no, not, don't)* are great examples of this phenomenon.

The earliest way that a toddler "asks a question" is to raise his pitch at the end of the word. For example, if a toddler says *Daddy gone* with a falling, rather emphatic tone, he's probably using that sentence to tell you that his dad is indeed not present. On the other hand, if a toddler says those same words with a rising tone at the end, he's probably asking whether his dad is gone or not. The key is that the toddler's meaning is not contained in just the words themselves. He's showing an understanding that speakers use inflection, or pitch changes, to also signal meaning. Toddlers don't jump from *Daddy gone?* to *Is Daddy gone?* instantly. They will first insert the word *is* in the middle and keep the rising inflection at the end to signal that the sentence is meant to be a question, *Daddy's gone?* Later, with development, they'll make that final necessary switch to move the word *is* to the beginning of the sentence, *Is Daddy gone?*

> The toddler's meaning is not contained in just the words themselves. He's showing an understanding that speakers use inflection, or pitch changes, to also signal meaning.

Negative forms also go through a metamorphosis from the time they emerge to the time they are used in an adult manner. Of course the earliest form is the ever popular *NO!* Toddlers initially use this word to "refuse"—that is, to *refuse* a request to share a toy, to *refuse* a request to go to sleep, to *refuse* the request to eat some vegetables. During this stage of development, you'll hear your toddler use the word *no* and other negatives, such as *not*, in other ways. Imagine a toddler putting his hand into a toy box to find a toy cow, but instead he pulls out a toy horse. The path to the sophisticated sentence "This isn't a cow" begins with a simple *no* (as the toddler shakes his head, throws the toy horse aside, and continues to reach into the box). He says *no* as if to say, "This is not what I expected!" Later he might say, *no cow* or *not cow*. Later, he'll add the words *this* and *a*; *this not a cow*. Finally, he'll insert the word *is* for the final version. . . . *This isn't a cow*.

Sentence Complexity

The complexity of a sentence is determined primarily by the verb(s) involved. As we said earlier, during this stage of development toddlers progress from simple verbs such as *go* or *run* to more complex verbs such as *think* or *promise*. With these changes come changes in the complexity of the entire sentence. Just as single words turn into simple sentences, so do simple sentences turn into complex sentences that contain more than one verb. Initially, you'll hear sentences with the 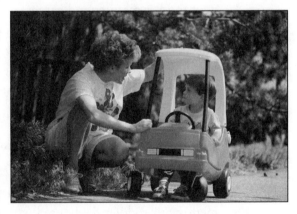 word *and* or *then* between the verbs, such as "I jump and run," "Sit down and play," "Pick this one, then get this one." These changes in sentence forms reflect not only the toddler's increasing language skills, but also her increasing ability to talk about events in the past or future. Later she'll display her understanding of cause-effect relationships by using sentences such as, "He's crying because he lost the toy." Toward the end of your toddler's third year of life, the verbs that represent advanced concepts also will be used in longer sentences, such as "I didn't see her do it," or "I think she's pretty," or "Mommy said to go."

Using Groups of Sentences

Just as your toddler is learning to link ideas within sentences, so too is he starting to link ideas *across* sentences. Around age three, toddlers begin talking about events using two or three sentences that are related to the same topic. For example, a toddler might talk about a snack time event by saying, "We eat popcorn. We watch TV. We drink juice." These sentences, although they might not be in the exact order the actions took place, demonstrate the toddler's understanding that those actions together represented a situation or event experienced. As your toddler matures and garners more experiences with familiar events, you will find that the actions discussed will be in the right time order as well. This ability to talk about situations in the correct time sequence will lay the groundwork for your toddler's ability to tell and understand stories in the next few years.

What About Speech Development?

DURING THE BABBLING and first word stages of development, your toddler likely used words with speech sounds that are relatively easier to produce, such as *p, b, n,* and *w.* As we said in chapters 1 and 2, most of his productions were probably one-syllable words, with some two-syllable words used occasionally. Now, you'll see all of the other speech sounds appear in the words he uses. During this stage of language development, your toddler will make astounding progress in the area of speech. During the second year of life, you probably had to interpret at least half of what he said to those nice strangers in the grocery store or even the grandparents. However, your toddler's speech will improve to be almost completely understandable by everyone. Researchers in toddler speech development have found that most three-year-olds are understandable about 75 percent of the time. By age four, this increases to 90 percent or even higher.

> The ability to talk about situations in the correct time sequence will lay the groundwork for your toddler's ability to tell and understand stories in the next few years.

Typical "Errors"

YOU KNOW THAT when toddlers begin talking, their production of phrases such as *little red wagon* will not be totally correct in terms of speech sound use. Let's face it—some sounds and words are just harder to say than others. Yet, toddlers will need some of those tricky words in order to communicate. In chapter 2, we talked about how some one-year-olds may actually avoid words that contain sounds that are harder to make. However, two- and three-year-olds can't "afford" to keep avoiding words—they just have too much to say!

So, what's the toddler to do with this "mismatch" between her ability to articulate and the difficulty of words that she wants to use? Well, she does the best she can. The young two-year-old might leave off final sounds (*si* for *sit*) or syllables (*e-fant* for *elephant*). Later these word parts will be included, but she'll still leave off parts of consonant blends (two or more consonants said together), such as saying *tick* for *stick* and *bu* for *blue*. In addition to deleting speech sounds, toddlers also substitute easier sounds for harder ones. It is easier for most toddlers to make the *t, d, p, b, m, n,* and *w* speech sounds and harder to make the *k, g, s, z, sh, ch, j, r,* and *l* sounds. Consequently, you're likely to hear your toddler substituting sounds from the first group for speech sounds for those in the last group.

It's important to keep in mind that your toddler should be moving from deleting sounds to substituting sounds to using correct sounds. Although many of the two-year-old's "errors" will be deletions, by the time she is three most of her "errors" should be substitutions. Further, some substitutions are cause for more concern than others. For example, substituting a *th* sound for an *s* sound wouldn't necessarily be a cause for concern in a three-year-old. However, substituting a *w* sound for the *s* would. In chapter 9, we will be discussing what you can do if you're worried about whether your toddler's speech sound errors might be signals of a potential problem.

Social Language Skills

YOU WILL SEE major changes in your toddler's ability to use language to interact with those around him during his toddler years. One of the main reasons for this increase is that the other areas of language (speech sounds, word and sentence use) become so much better. It's easier to carry on a conversation with someone you can understand! Your toddler can tell you what's on his mind more effectively because he knows more words and can use better grammar.

At the same time, there are specific changes that occur as a result of your toddler's increasing knowledge about communication interactions. We get a lot of "unspoken" clues from people during conversations. For example, we know that eye contact usually means that the person that we're talking to is listening, and conversely, a lack of eye contact, or looking away, typically means that the person isn't interested in carrying the conversation further. We also know to wait until our partner stops talking before making our own comments. Your toddler will begin to pick up on these clues, too. A busy parent will often hear, "Mommy, look at me!" when she is trying to continue doing household chores while her toddler is telling her something! Such requests offer evidence for the toddler's appreciation of the role that eye contact plays in conversational exchanges.

As we said in chapter 2, babies use words that refer to the "here and now." They talk about people, things, and events that are occurring at that time, in that place. Toddlers, on the other hand, begin to use language to talk about past or future events and about things or people that aren't in their immediate environment.

Toddlers first use language referring to the past, or the "there and then," by discussing familiar events that tend to be associated with common routines. We call these "scripted events." For example, most toddlers become familiar with a certain routine for bedtime, bath time, and later, birthday parties and fast-food restaurants.

> Your toddler should be moving from deleting sounds to substituting sounds to using correct sounds.

Having a script for an event allows your toddler to "concentrate" more on what happens during that time, making it easier to learn the new language involved in that situation. He can predict how actions occur and what objects should be used, and thus, he can attend to the details of the situation. However, these expectations for what *should* occur may sometimes cause this finer, detailed learning to not occur if those expectations are not met. For example, when Nick was young, he had a script for birthday parties that involved, besides cake and presents, breaking open a piñata. This occurred because the first few birthday parties he attended had this activity. When he attended his first "non-piñata" party, he was unsure what to think and spent a great deal of time wondering about the piñata rather than learning what he could from the party. This example is given not to encourage you to never have variations in the activities in which your toddler is involved; rather, it is used to explain why some toddlers may not seem to understand or learn as much from one experience as they might from others.

Toddlers also begin to make more and more comments that relate to what their conversational partner, the person to whom they are speaking, said beforehand. During the one-word stage, babies pretty much "run the show." If the baby's one-word sentence relates to his conversational partner's, it's because the partner is following the *baby's* lead, not vice versa. Toddlers, on the other hand, do follow their partner's lead at times and comment on what was said before they add new information to the conversation. Additionally, toddlers are able to contribute more to conversations, sometimes saying two or three sentences before their partner says something else.

One of our favorite developmental changes during the third and fourth years of life involves the way toddlers talk differently based on their conversational partner. Older children and adults have many different styles or ways of speaking, and they use the style that is most fitting for a given situation. For example, you might use one style of conversing with a potential business client or your boss (respectful, formal, polite, reserved) and a different style if conversing with a close friend (chatty, informal, slang). During the toddler years, we begin to see a glimpse of this style change across conversational situations. In chapter 2, we talked about a special language style or register called child-directed speech (CDS). Interestingly, toddlers often use a different register when speaking to babies or animals. They tend to use a higher pitch with a more singsong rhythm. In other words, they use aspects of CDS. At the end of the toddler period, many toddlers use a third register for speaking to adults. Their language may be a little more formal, polite, or complex when speaking to an adult than when speaking to a peer.

When two or more individuals are talking, invariably there is a need for one of the individuals to clarify, or restate, what he has just said. Typically, this occurs when another individual asks him to clarify, using either gestures (a perplexed look) or language (What? Where did he go? Who did that?). Your toddler is starting to learn how to use both of these skills. On the one hand, she is learning to ask for clarification. She may do this by saying "What? Huh?," or by scrunching up her face. On the flip side, she also is learning, during these third and fourth years of life, to clarify or revise what she has said when her conversational partner is confused. Initially, she will do this by saying the same word or words again, but attempting to articulate them more precisely, such as the following:

> Toddlers often use a different register when speaking to babies or animals. They tend to use a higher pitch with a more singsong rhythm.

Child: "A fit."
Mother: "A what?"
Child: "A fish."

Soon, she will develop an additional strategy for clarifying her language. In addition to saying the word more accurately, she will know how to substitute a word for the word in question, such as the following:

Child: "I got a Ranger."
Friend: "What did you get?"
Child: "A car. A Ranger."

There are two final developments that occur in the area of social language during the toddler years worth noting. Have you ever considered how tricky it would be to explain to another person when to use terms such as *I/you, mine/yours,* and *here/there?* There's a technical word for such terms, *deixis,* and it refers to words that change depending on the perspective of the speaker. For example, when a mother refers to her shoe, she says "my shoe"; yet everyone else who wants to talk about her shoe must say "your shoe." It's a clear case of different words being used to refer to exactly the same thing. However, they can't be interchanged. The mother can't refer to her shoe as "your shoe" and no one else can call it "my shoe." Yet, when referring to some other specific shoe, Mom must say "your shoe" and someone else out there must say "my shoe." We warn you—thinking about such things can give you a headache if you do it too long! Our point here is that toddlers seem to rather effortlessly understand and employ this principle of changing words depending on the person or location. They rarely confuse such terms. Isn't that amazing and quite impressive?

The final example of your toddler's incredible ingenuity as a language learner is in the area of ellipsis. This word, *ellipsis,* refers to leaving unnecessary words out of your sentences. Consider the following scenario:

Customer: "I'll have the steak with a baked potato and salad."

Waiter: "How would you like that cooked?"

Customer: "Medium rare."

Waiter: "What kind of dressing would you like?"

Customer: "Ranch."

Waiter: "Do you want butter and sour cream?"

Customer: "Only butter."

Both of these speakers are using ellipsis throughout this exchange. Each speaker chooses words to include or exclude based on what he expects the other person to know or what's already happened in the conversation. Here's how the same exchange might look without ellipsis:

Customer: "For my meal, I would like you to ask the chef to prepare a steak, baked potato, and salad. When they're ready, I'd like you to bring them to my table so that I can eat them."

Waiter: "I'll certainly take care of sharing your order with the chef and then transporting the food back to your table. However, first I have some questions for you. Your steak can be cooked to several levels of doneness—including well done, medium, medium rare, and rare. Which level would you prefer?"

Customer: "I'd like my steak cooked to the medium-rare level of doneness."

Waiter: "You're having a salad and salads are usually served with dressing, which is a liquid-like substance that is mixed in with the salad. We have six kinds of dressing: French, Thousand Island, Italian, blue cheese, ranch, and honey mustard. What kind of dressing would you like with your salad?"

Customer: "I'd like ranch dressing to be mixed in with my salad."

Waiter: "Customers often like to put butter, sour cream, and even chives on their baked potatoes. Do you want any of these extras?"

Customer: "I only want butter for my baked potato. I don't want sour cream or chives."

Obviously, this second exchange would be ridiculous. Frankly, it would waste time and waste words. Toddlers pick up on this quite early in their lives. In fact, perhaps the *only* times toddlers violate this use of ellipsis is when well-meaning but misguided adults ask toddlers to "say the whole thing" when a child has been asked a question ("Where will you go?") and the child answers appropriately with an elliptical answer ("to the store"). There is one obvious point to be made here, then. Don't expect toddlers, or anyone for that matter, to answer questions like this with anything but an appropriate, shortened version of the answer.

Helping Your Toddler Build Language

DURING THIS PERIOD of language development, perhaps more than in any period of his life thus far, you will see leaps and bounds in what your toddler is learning to say. If you are like us, you will be constantly amazed at what your toddler can express on his own. He seems to be a sponge, soaking up everything that people are saying and then using similar ideas, sentence structures, and vocabulary words in new and creative ways. You are a major source of knowledge and learning for your toddler. Almost anywhere and anytime, you will be providing the fertilizer for his blossoming skills. Let's talk about some specific ideas to show you the effect you can have on your toddler's development.

Reading Time

We know you've been reading to your toddler for some time. As you undoubtedly have been discovering as he matures, his capacity to sit and listen to your book reading, and his ability to understand more complicated stories, is increasing. For toddlers, your book selections should be moving away from picture books that encourage labeling and moving toward books that involve some type of sequence of events. Many times, these books represent events that occur in your toddler's life. Book reading now will help your toddler learn more than just words. By reading these types of books to your toddler, you

you've been trying to follow your toddler's lead, focusing on the topics in which she is interested, and commenting on her actions and words. As you run around, trying to follow this rule of thumb, we have some other suggestions for you to consider that reflect the new language skills your toddler is acquiring.

First, as in all phases of development, you want to be a good modeler of language. This means that when your toddler says a word, phrase, or whole sentence, you want to expand on what she has said. So, if your toddler says, "I like candy," you can say, "You like candy? Yeah, you like all kinds of candy, don't you?" or something to that effect. Remember, by focusing on your toddler's ideas, and expanding on those ideas, you are showing her what she says is important and that she can say even more as her communication skills increase.

Playtime also is an excellent time to expose your toddler to new words and phrases. This will happen naturally. As you play with your toddler, it will be tempting to move into a "teaching mode." With such a sponge, it seems only appropriate to teach and then test what she is learning. Many parents at this point try, either because it seems appropriate or, more likely, because they feel pressure from relatives or the media, to teach certain concepts, such as colors, opposites, and letters, to name a few. While your toddler most definitely needs to learn these concepts, *how* she learns them may be very natural or unnatural, depending on the process.

Take, for example, opposite word pairs, such as *hot* and *cold*, *up* and *down*, *big* and *little*. When toddlers are learning these types of words, they typically do not learn them together. That would indeed be a difficult task. To understand opposite pair words, a toddler must understand that the word pair represents a continuum, a progression of that concept, and that each word represents one end of that continuum. For *hot* and *cold*, a toddler must understand that both words represent temperature, and that *hot* is at one end of that continuum of heat while *cold* is the other end. Thus, because of this difficult

task, most toddlers will learn to talk about the concept (temperature) with one of the opposite words *(hot)* before they
begin to use the opposite word. In fact, before acquiring the
second member of that pair, many toddlers will either refrain
from referring to the other end of the continuum or use a
phrase such as *not-hot* or *no-big,* and so forth.

Like opposites, the same can be said for color terms. During
the second and third years of life, many toddlers are developing
an understand that words like *red, green,* and *yellow* refer to the
color or hue of items. When you think about it, this is no easy
task. Color is not an easy concept to talk about, especially because of the great variability in shades (just think about all the
different shades of blue in our world). Thus, initially, all your
toddler may know about color words is that they are to be used
to talk about a feature of an object. Because of this, it is not uncommon for toddlers to label a red sweater as "the blue one."
Knowing that your child has already accomplished the great
feat of talking about color may help keep you from panicking
that your toddler is color blind or won't be ready for school,
even though she is only two or three years old.

Finally, letters of the alphabet are particular targets of
parental teaching. We would never argue against helping your
child learn the letters of the alphabet. As you will see in the
next chapter, knowledge of letter names, and the sounds they
make, is highly important. But the same caution about teaching that we gave for other concepts above is true for letter
learning as well. Incorporate letters into play instead of drilling
your toddler.

So, what are we suggesting you do during playtime? Just as
the word suggests, during playtime, *play* with your toddler.
You can't teach your toddler language, and language is not just
colors, numbers, letters, and specific concepts like hot and
cold. Incorporate these concepts into play, versus making them
the focus of a specific activity, unless your toddler shows a preference for this. When you are playing trucks and cars with

your toddler, your expansions of his words and phrases can include the color word for that object ("Go truck? Yes, there goes the yellow truck."). You can line up the cars in the garage, confirming you have all of them together ("One, two, three trucks. Yep, they are all here."). You can even comment on similarities in the letters seen on toys ("Look! This truck has a *T* on the license plate, just like this one does."). Of course, there is nothing wrong with singing songs or saying rhymes that involve these concepts, because, again, the focus is on fun and play rather than on showing success on a parent-devised test. As we state in our major points in chapter 1: Facilitate language development, don't teach it.

Outing Times

As you can probably guess, the strategies we have talked about for book reading and playtime are equally useful for times when you go out on the town with your toddler. There are additional strategies you can use during these times, though, that may help strengthen your toddler's understanding and communication of events.

The first time your toddler experiences an event (her first time to eat at a restaurant, her first movie, or her first trip to the circus), all the new people, objects, and actions that she is experiencing can be somewhat overwhelming. Remember your first day in high school or college? It probably was somewhat confusing. What you were supposed to do? What were all the papers you were given called? If you had been required to talk about that first day, we bet it would not have been an easy task. The same is true for your child. However, you can make these initial experiences easier for your toddler to learn and discuss. Before you go to a new place, talk about what will happen. As you are involved in the actual event, discuss with your toddler what is happening. After the event is over, revisit it and remember aloud with your child all the people, objects, and actions that occurred. Finally, do this frequently for the same event. Through repeated exposures and experiences, your toddler will develop a better understanding of the important components of these events, the actions that occur, and how they occur, which will enable her to share this information in a more logical, correctly ordered manner.

Chapter Summary

DURING THE SECOND and third years of life, your toddler has completed a great accomplishment: She has cracked the code for building sentences; she has developed excellent strategies for being a conversationalist; she says her speech sounds correctly. Through your guidance and care, coupled with your knowledge of how language develops, you have helped her along that path of learning. She now is preparing to move into another important phase of the language-learning process. In chapter 4, you will not only learn what else she is developing for her spoken language skills, but you will begin to understand what you can do to help her in the development of her written language skills: reading and writing. Are you as ready as she will be?

4

From Spoken to
Written Language:
Setting Your Preschooler
on the Right Path

DID YOU KNOW?

- Five-year-old children are like mini-adults in their speech and language skills.
- Kindergarten children tell stories with actual plots.
- Rhyming is an important building block for reading.

*E*llen and Joe both worked out of the home. They had the usual challenges of hardworking parents trying to hold down their jobs while raising their five-year-old daughter. Life was hectic. They worried that they didn't spend enough time with Annie to teach her what she needed to know before going into kindergarten. Sure, they read to her at night, but was that enough? They felt guilty because the time spent with her involved doing everyday routines or errands, with only some time devoted to direct play *with her. Because of this guilt, they invented special games or activities to make up for lost "quality" time. When Ellen had to take Annie grocery shopping instead of staying home and reading, she made up a game of having Annie cross out the items as Ellen put them in the cart. When Joe felt guilty writing the bills instead of playing with Annie, he had her help put stamps on the envelopes to keep her occupied. When the parents took their daughter to the kindergarten screening day, they were nervous that the teachers would find she knew less than her peers. Imagine their shock when the teachers marveled that Annie knew some of her letters and how to "read" from left to right. Ellen and Joe hadn't taught Annie these things. How did she learn all of this?*

Your child has learned an incredible amount of language by the time he turns four. In fact, as you will see, he is soon to be considered "adultlike" in the complexity of his sentence structure and in the ways he interacts with others. His vocabulary continues to become more sophisticated and varied. As your child blossoms into a true conversationalist, you will find that you begin to emphasize another aspect of language, one that you know will be needed as your child enters formal schooling. This new area of language will be the written word.

Although we have talked mostly about what your child is learning about spoken language, and will continue to do that in this chapter, you will find that your child is also beginning to show signs of learning about reading and writing. Some of this learning may be overt. She may "read" books, saying sentences word for word as you have read them in her favorite book a thousand times. She may also begin to write her name or other simple words that she sees frequently. She is acquiring some other skills that will help her with written language; they may not be as obvious, yet they are equally important. These skills include learning to rhyme, knowing the names of letters, and so on. Thus, this chapter will cover not only what other spoken language skills your child is learning during these years, but also what she is learning about written language that will help her as she begins to read, write, and spell. And we will show how parents can prepare their children for these "academic" skills in easy, everyday activities. So much being learned, so much you can do to help your child!

Further Developing Spoken Language Skills

DURING HER FOURTH and fifth years, your preschooler will be refining certain language skills she has been using for some time while also learning new spoken language skills. These new developments occur in all areas of language, including semantics (meaning), speech sounds, grammar, and social language skills.

Sentence Structure and Grammar

Your child's sentence structures should be quite varied and complex at this age. Many of his sentences should contain more than one verb, such as "I want to go now!" or "I know how to do that." Your child's use of these sentences and his understanding of them are important for several reasons. First, when your child uses these types of sentences, it allows him to convey much more information within shorter amounts of time. More complex relationships among thoughts can be expressed. In addition, within about three years, your child will be reading complex sentences in books. With solid understanding and use of these types of sentences, his ability to understand them when he reads will be enhanced.

> She may "read" books, saying sentences word for word as you have read them in her favorite book a thousand times.

Along with sentence structure, you also will hear your child use word endings that sound quite mature. Even though your child has been using special endings on words for a year or so, such as the *-ing* ("I'm eating."), the *-s* ("He jumps." "Billy's swimming."), and the *-ed* ("She walked to the park."), new and more advanced word beginnings and endings will develop. A good example of this occurred one day when Nick was asking his dad to wind up a toy motorcycle. Having discussed that each time the motorcycle raced across the floor, it was "rad," he turned to his dad and asked him to wind it up again so that it would go "radly." This example actually demonstrates two points. Nick was learning to attach the *-ly*, an ending that is learned during these years to change an adjective or noun (*friend*) to an adverb (*friendly*). This example also demonstrates another point we have made and will continue to make throughout this book: Your preschooler is not just a little robot, imitating everything you say. Rather, your preschooler is actively learning the rules of speech and language, constructing the rules based on what he hears every day. What a genius!

Speech Sounds

Your preschooler's speech skills also are nearing adult level. She continues to be highly understandable to others. True, she may still be trying to correctly produce her *r*, but she has mastered other difficult sounds like *s, z, ch, sh,* and consonant combinations, such as *st, ms,* and the like. By the end of their sixth year, most children will have even corrected their *r*. Children in their fourth and fifth years still may "trip up" on longer words, words that have several syllables in them, like *Cinderella, spaghetti,* and *aluminum*. But seriously, how many of us still say *cimmanon* for cinnamon?

Vocabulary

As in the previous four years, your child's vocabulary continues to grow by leaps and bounds every day. In fact, vocabulary development will likely never stop. (We bet you have even learned some new words reading this book!) But your child's development in vocabulary this year is more than just new words. He is increasing his ability to express new meanings. For example, he now is able to use verbs that express communication acts, such as *tell, say,* and *talk*. While this may seem insignificant, it is actually quite important. Not only can your child use this new meaning to tattle ("I'm telling Mommy!" "He said a bad word!"), but it also allows your child to talk about language itself, a skill we will address later in this chapter.

Finally, your child is expanding his meanings of words that he already has learned. For example, your child may have learned the word *first* in relation to his older brother's grade in school. Now, he is learning that the same word can signify other mean-

> He now begins to use language in different ways, often as subtle ways to get what he wants!

ings, such as being first in line or the first word of a book. Taken as a whole, then, your child's meaning system, semantics, is not only growing in size, but it is deepening in meaning as well. Amazing, isn't it?

Social Language Skills

Perhaps more than in any other area of language, this year your child is really refining his social language skills. While he has already begun using appropriate eye contact, topic skills, and turn-taking skills, he now begins to use language in different ways, often as subtle ways to get what he wants! Children who are four and five years old are developing the ability to use indirect language and hints. These language skills involve implying a certain meaning even when the words used do not state that meaning. A common example is the use of "politeness forms" when requesting an object. For example, during this time your child will learn to ask for music by saying, "Can I turn on the radio?" Now, even though the ornery parent or two may say, "I don't know, can you," we all know that your child is not asking whether he has the potential to turn on the radio. Rather, he is expressing his wants. Because your preschooler has learned that "softening" requests often gets him better results, he begins to construct these types of sentences. Sometimes it seems that these sentences happen more with others than with his own mom and dad. You may experience times when a neighbor or friend says, "Your daughter is so polite. She always asks for things in such a nice way." And you feel yourself asking, "Who? My daughter?"

Besides demonstrating politeness, skills such as using hints and indirect language also allow children to say what they want to say, without saying it specifically. When Nick was four years of age, he was being particularly stubborn about wearing his parka zipped up to the neck. Because it was bitterly cold outside, his mother kept insisting that it be zipped. After battling back and forth (he would unzip, she would insist he zip it up), she stated that he would need to go inside if he unzipped one more time. Not wishing to go inside, but still needing to express how he felt, he waited a minute, and then began to verbalized his aversion to the jacket: "Ahem, mmm, boy, this jacket is tight. . . . (cough) . . . This jacket makes it hard to breathe . . . (hack)." Through his indirect language and his hinting, he was able to express his dislike of the situation and yet still play outside. As your child reaches this age, you will soon see how he can masterfully manipulate language to meet his needs. And you were excited when he said his first word!

Your child also is developing a much more sophisticated way of responding to requests for clarification. Recall that this skill is highly important for maintaining a conversation. If one person in a conversation asks for clarification and the other person does not respond with an understandable or useful clarification, the conversation goes nowhere (but down-hill, that is). Up until now, your child should have been using two highly effective clarification strategies: changing how he says a word (saying it more clearly) and changing the word in question to an easier-to-understand word. Now, during his fourth and fifth years of life, he should be adding a new strategy to his arsenal. When asked to clarify what he just said, your child should also be able to change the whole sentence structure to help another person understand. For example, when Genevieve was four, she was talking to her parents in the car. Noticing a particularly beautiful mountain range out her window, she said, "Look at the Canadia mountains!" Her parents, not quite understanding her, said, "What?" She replied: "Those mountains over there. The Canadia ones. Look at them." Thus, she was able to help her listener under-stand what she was saying and the conversation continued successfully.

As your child develops in her fourth and fifth years, other social language skills that continue to develop and mature in-clude her ability to maintain a topic (without your help, that is) and move from topic to topic with very subtle yet under-standable ways. This latter skill, sometimes called topic shad-ing, usually occurs when an individual is talking with someone with whom she is quite familiar. For example, "listen" to the following conversation, which occurred in the car between Caitlin and her friend, Audrey. Notice how many different topics are covered, yet the movement from one topic to an-other is very subtle.

Caitlin: "I want to get some new shoes at the mall."

Audrey: "Me, too. I saw some new shoes on TV."

Caitlin: "Yeah, and you know what else? I also saw they have new surprises in Kids' Meals at McDonald's."

Audrey: "Yeah, you know, Joey really likes McDonald's, mostly because of the play area."

Caitlin: "I like that play area, too. Joey is really into Power Ranger stuff, huh?"

Audrey: "Uh-huh. Some of them are cute, but not as cute as Miss Kitty stuff."

Caitlin: "Oh, that's my favoritest thing. We went to Seattle and I went to a whole store that had that. Seattle is a fun place to go."

Audrey: "I love going to Seattle because we always stop and get a TCBY on the way down."

Caitlin: "Yummy! My favorite flavor there is white chocolate. What about you?"

Audrey: "My favorite is double-Dutch chocolate."

As you can see, these two friends had quite the conversation. While some may listen to this and be amused about the constant "chatter" between the two young girls, one can look at this short conversational excerpt and actually see how sophisticated it is. Both children took responsibility for keeping the conversation going. Both easily segued from one topic to another. In total, there were five topics covered (the mall/shoes, McDonald's, Joey, Seattle, and TCBY), but because each friend relied on her knowledge of the other and what she already knew, the movement from one topic to the next was smooth and hardly noticeable. In situations such as this, you as a parent are able to view firsthand the incredible social language skills that your child is acquiring and using.

Storytelling Skills

IN CHAPTER 3, we talked about your child's ability to link several thoughts and sentences about an event in a time-ordered fashion. Now, during years four and five, she will begin to expand on this ability. Around the age of five, your child will begin to show some cause and effect in the stories she tells. In other words, there will seem to be a "plot" to her stories or descriptions of experiences she has had. At first, however, this will occur only when she's talking about events with which she has had lots of experiences. Let's provide an example. Consider this story told by Genevieve when she was five. She was asked to tell a story about some children who went to a jungle. She said:

"Once upon a time, there was two kids who went to a jungle. And when they came to the jungle, they had to pay some money. So they didn't have any money, so they went home, get some money, steal money from their mom's purse, come back to the . . . zoo and give him the money and he would give them some food to feed the animals. So they walked along and then that's the end."

> Around the age of five, there will seem to be a "plot" to her stories or descriptions of experiences she has had.

As you can read in this example, Genevieve's story has a plot, a cause and effect. In her story, the problem, which was the lack of money, caused the children to get the money, which caused them to be able to get some animal food. This story was not only in the correct time sequence, but it also had the more mature cause and effect that most adults are expecting to hear in a story such as this. One could argue that this story was pretty advanced for someone of Genevieve's age (and her father would agree!), because she was talking about a topic that was not that familiar to her: going to a jungle. But notice what she did. She turned the topic into one with which she had more experience: going to the zoo. (Of course, the hope is that the particular segment about stealing from the mother's purse was *unfamiliar*!) Your preschooler will continue to grow in her storytelling abilities, as well as her general ability to talk about events, as she matures. Her stories will become more detailed and longer and will include more plots, not unlike the daytime soap operas on TV. As parents of teenagers, we can attest to the fact that, with age, stories become much more complicated. But that's another book!

Helping Your Preschooler Refine His Spoken Language Skills

AS WE SAID earlier, your child is an active constructor of knowledge, figuring out most of the rules of language without your telling him. Granted, this probably would not happen if you weren't such a good model. And so, during the fourth and fifth years, you should continue to do what you have done in the past. Be an active listener and participant in the conversations he wants to have. Follow his lead in conversations, asking open-ended questions ("Tell me more.") that encourage him to elaborate on his topics. If he is still learning to produce certain sounds, provide good, accurate models of words containing the sounds he is misarticulating, without asking him to repeat the words. Talk daily about events and happenings in your life, so he can understand how people tend to talk about situations, especially when there is a causal aspect to the action (problem, action, solution). Remember, your role is not to sit down and teach your child language (could any of us stand to do that?). Instead, your role is to provide lots of good models of speech and language, using encouraging and supportive comments and feedback that create an atmosphere of trust, love, and understanding. This is the context in which we all want to learn, especially children. If you provide this kind of atmosphere, your child should find it much easier to grasp how he is supposed to communicate.

A "New" Language

By the time your child is five years of age, most language experts will say that she is "adultlike" in her spoken language skills. We agree with this. As you can see from the examples provided above, she has become quite the conversationalist. She has taken on the formidable task of learning how to communicate and made the task look easy. She now is gearing up for another difficult task, one that will lay the foundation for everything she does in school. She is getting ready to read and write. In her fourth and fifth years, your child will start to learn about written language in ways that will serve her well as she starts to learn to read, write, and spell.

The second half of this chapter will describe what she is learning about literacy during these years, how this knowledge will help your child when she starts to read and write, and what you can do as a parent to help her in that learning. You likely will notice something else different about how children learn this type of language. Whereas spoken language was learned implicitly; that is, your child was picking up the rules of speech and language without any direct attention or teaching from you about those rules, when it comes to written language, your child will require active attention, instruction, and directed play to acquire this aspect of language. And you can serve as an instructor while continuing to make the learning fun and exciting.

Developing Foundational Skills for Literacy

During the first five years of life, your child is learning to speak language. However, ask him to talk or think about language he is learning, and he most likely will be stymied. What do we mean talk about language? Talking and thinking about language, often referred to as metalinguistics, means being able to treat our words, sentences, and rules of language as the topic of conversation. When we talk about how many words are in a sentence, we are talking about language. When we discuss how another individual has an "accent," we are talking about language. When we talk about a definition of a word, we are talking about language. All of these situations demonstrate metalinguistics, thinking and talking about language. Children five and under show limited abilities to do this metalinguistic thinking and talking.

> As you read to her and point to the pictures or the words on the page, she is learning the differences between pictures and words.

During years three and four, your toddler may be showing some precursory skills to metalinguistics, such as using rhyming words or talking about the "funny way" certain people talk. But it won't be until he is closer to six years of age that he begins to understand how one can talk about language itself as a specific topic. Nevertheless, these precursory metalinguistic skills are helping to lay the foundation for later developing literacy skills. Let's talk about some specific skills.

Knowledge About Print

We hope you've been reading to your preschooler since she was a baby. As you have been reading, you have been talking about the pictures, relating them to your preschooler's life, and providing lots of readings of her favorite books. Perhaps you have noticed lately that your preschooler is starting to make comments about the books you read. She may be pointing to pictures of words you read. She may be tracing the sentences or words with her finger as you read them or as she "pretend" reads. You might observe her trying to write words, asking for letters. She might have even commented on how long her name is (Genevieve) versus her other friend's (Mary). All of these comments and actions are signs that your preschooler is learning about print, the "stuff" that is written language. This developing knowledge will be a crucial component to developing her reading and writing skills. And the great thing about this is that you have played an important role in causing this to happen.

Book Reading

During book reading times, your preschooler will be learning a great deal about books and how they are used that you take for granted. For example, by watching you as you read to her, she is learning how to hold a book, how to turn pages, where the first page is, and how to wait until you are finished reading a page to turn to the next one. As you read to her and point to the pictures or the words on the page, she is learning the differences between pictures and words, how the "white spaces" between the groups of letters represent the end of one word and the beginning of the next, and that the book or reading material dictates to a great extent what words are said. In other words, the book establishes the topic of the conversation. Most parents and adults take these concepts for granted, but they are new to your preschooler and must be learned before she picks up a book to read for herself.

High-Print Environments

When children are in their third, fourth, and fifth years of life, they are not only noticing the objects and people around them, they also are beginning to notice that older individuals use certain objects to communicate with others. They see mom writing a note to an older brother and pinning it on the refrigerator, and they then see the older brother reading the note and performing a chore. They see dad making a grocery list and then using it at the grocery store. They see parents and siblings reading magazines, newspapers, bank statements, and school books. They see family members typing on the computer and printing out their written product.

What are all these actions showing? Your preschooler is learning that language can be relayed via other modes of communication *and* he is seeing that there is a purpose to these actions. Preschoolers who see others using the "tools" of written language (pencils, pens, paper, computers, books, and so forth) and how and why they are used (to remind, to inform, to pay, and so on) are learning about printed or written language. These types of home environments are called "high-print" environments because they facilitate the preschooler's ability to understand how and why printed material can be used to communicate. So, next time you head off to the hardware store, take your preschooler with you. Show him your list. Point out each item as it is purchased and let him check it off the list. You are helping him learn a great deal about written language and you've got a great conversational partner with you as well.

> Follow his lead in conversations, asking open-ended questions ("Tell me more.") that encourage him to elaborate on his topics.

Letter Knowledge

Children as young as three may have some idea that letters represent language and that strings of them are generally used to write down language. It is not uncommon to see three- and four-year-old toddlers attempting to write letters on their artwork or a "letter to Daddy." As children reach the age of five, they have a much better idea of what letters represent. Coinciding with this is their growing understanding of letter names and letter-sound relationships.

As your preschooler enters her sixth year of life, and as she is exposed to more book reading and additional high-print experiences, she will begin to actively use her knowledge of letter names and letter-sound relationships to write language on paper. Letter-name knowledge involves knowing the names of letters when she sees them. Letter-sound relationship means knowing the sound, or sounds, that a letter can make. Most preschoolers learn these letter names early by reading alphabet books or being actively taught letters by their parents. When preschoolers come from high-print environments, they also tend to learn about the "power" of letters: how letters stand for language, how to write them, and how letters differ from other scribbles and scratches made on paper. Encourage your preschooler to express herself in any way she chooses to write. While her inventions in word spellings may seem random or incorrect, she is learning and demonstrating a great deal of knowledge about written language.

Knowledge About Words

Your preschooler has learned many new words since he spoke his first word at the age of one. Indeed, there may be some words you wished he had not learned! However, as good as he is at using a variety of words, he is less able to think and talk about those words, such as defining them, what they look like, and how they are written. Let's go over a few examples.

Most children, before five or six, will be able to use a word or phrase but not be able to define or explain it when questioned. When Nick was three years old, he was playing with his dad, and suddenly said, "Cut it out." When asked what "cut it out" meant, he was unable to answer, even though he had just used that particular phrase correctly and appropriately. When his dad said, "Do you mean, cut it out, like with scissors?" he responded, "Yes." He was unable to think about what he was talking about, much less understand, the dual meaning of the words he was using.

Children before the age of five or six also have a difficult time separating an object from the name of the object. It seems for children in the first four to five years of life, the word that stands for an object is actually considered to be part of the object. For example, when a younger child is asked what a long word is, a typical response might be *hose* or *train* or even *alligator*. In the child's mind, the length of the object represents the length of the word. Using the one of the examples above, *train* would be called a long word because the physical item, train, has many cars attached to it. Thus, the child is not thinking about the word itself (how long it takes to say it, how many letters we use to write it) but rather what the object it represents looks like. You may even see this same confusion in your preschooler's early attempts at spelling. He may spell his dad's name with many letters, but his baby sister's name with only one or two. After all, his dad is bigger so his name should contain more letters. On the other hand, his sister is small so her name should contain only a few letters. Although your preschooler may be making a mistake, his approach makes a lot of sense!

As he moves from his fifth year to his sixth year of life, you will find that your preschooler starts to recognize that words are separate from the objects to which they refer. He will begin to recognize that the length of a word, both in the way it sounds and is written, determines whether we call it long or short. This skill is highly important for literacy development. As he begins to write, his attempts to spell words will more closely represent what the word should look like. Ask your preschooler questions like, "What's a long word?" and "Why is *alligator* a long word?" You will be fascinated with his answer as

Remember, being able to think and talk about speech sounds is not the same as correctly using speech sounds.

you begin to determine where he is in developing his metalinguistic knowledge of words.

Knowledge About Sounds

This area of metalinguistics is probably the most crucial for children to learn. As you will see, without the ability to think and talk about the sounds of our language, a child is seriously at risk for experiencing difficulties learning to read and write. Remember, being able to think and talk about speech sounds is not the same as correctly using speech sounds (your preschooler has been doing that for a while). Rather, this area of new knowledge will involve actively talking about and playing with speech sounds and parts of words as one would play with a toy. This knowledge of sounds, most often referred to as phonological awareness, will develop gradually. The sequence of development is fairly similar for almost all children.

Initially, children first start treating the speech sounds of our language as toys when they catch on to rhyming. This may occur as early as three years of age. By five, however, it is expected that preschoolers can rhyme. Rhyming involves thinking of or recognizing two or more words that sound the same at the end of the word. For example, *cat, hat, pat,* and *rat* all rhyme. While this grouping of rhyming words might seem rather simplistic, for a preschooler to recognize this, she must be aware that all four of those words end with the same set of sounds: *at.* She must focus on the word, not the word meaning. This is not an easy task, which is why preschoolers develop these "preliteracy" skills much later than they do their spoken language skills. For example, when Nick was about three years of age, he seemed to have some understanding of rhyming, but was missing a crucial component. He would often approach someone (anyone who would listen!) and regale the person with his expertise in rhyming: "I can rhyme. Listen. Elephant. Elephant. See? They rhyme."

After rhyming, the next phonological awareness skill preschoolers generally develop involves knowing the number of words in a sentence. For example, a preschooler might recognize that "I like to eat sandwiches" contains five words. This skill might seem out of place in a discussion of preschoolers' phonological awareness, or knowledge of speech sounds, but it fits here. Perhaps the best way to understand this is to consider the times when you have heard someone speaking a different language than your own. For most of us, we think the person is a "quick talker" and we are hard pressed to understand where one word stops and another begins. This occurs because we are unfamiliar with the language, and we cannot use our knowledge of speech sounds to know which ones complete a word and which ones begin the next.

As your preschooler masters her ability to produce speech and language, she will begin to understand when a word stops and the next one begins. Using the example above, a preschooler without this understanding might say there are only four words in the sentence: I liketo eat sandwiches. In this case, the *to,* which carries very little meaning, is ignored. Similarly, another preschooler with less mature phonological awareness might say there are six words in the sentence: I like to eat sand wiches. Try this with your preschooler. If she is five, there is a good chance she will begin to "get it" and be able to count the number of words she hears in a simple sentence.

Children's phonological awareness continues to develop, such that they are able to count the number of syllables in words. Now, most preschoolers, and some adults, are not familiar with what a syllable is. However, if provided an example ("*Baby*"—clap, clap—"*Baby* has two claps in it!"), the preschooler with this phonological awareness skill will catch on.

These early phonological awareness skills lay the foundation for future phonological awareness skills that are crucial for reading and spelling. Later, when your child is about six or seven, she will be prepared to think about each speech sound in a word. The ability to do this, either to break up words into their individual speech sounds or to blend individual sounds together to form a word, is highly important for reading and spelling. That is, as a child begins to read in kindergarten or first grade, she will need to have some understanding that a series of letters represent sounds, and if you blend those sounds together *(c-a-t)*, you get a word. Also, your preschooler will need to learn that to spell a word, she needs to think about the individual sounds she hears in the word *(bath = b, a, th)*, and write down a letter or letters representing those sounds.

The skills discussed above, and the examples provided, help to reemphasize the difference between spoken and written language. When your preschooler was learning to speak, she didn't need to think about the sounds she was making. She didn't need to consider what a word was and whether it was represented by lots of letters or a few letters. However, as she begins to read and write, she will need to actively think about language. No wonder reading and spelling are such difficult tasks! For many children, they are the most challenging tasks of their entire school career. The positive side of this is that you have the potential to make that learning a bit easier. Let's talk about what you can do to ease this transition from learning spoken language to learning written language.

Helping Your Preschooler Learn About Literacy

THE SECOND HALF of this chapter discussed the many skills developing during the fifth and sixth years of life that can lay the groundwork for easier reading and writing development. Also, you have read that, unlike the development of spoken language, children need active, directed attention to written language to acquire these prerequisite skills. Does this mean you should be sitting down with your four- or five-year-old, quizzing him on his letters, and teaching him rhyming pairs of words? Of course not! Your preschooler wants you to be his parent, not his teacher. However, you can still help your preschooler attend to written language in a way that highlights the important ideas he needs to learn while making this learning fun, enjoyable, and part of everyday situations. You have an important role to play in helping your preschooler learn about written language, but there is no reason you both can't have fun learning. We provide you with some ideas, although undoubtedly, you will think of others.

There is one other important point to keep in mind, one that we have been emphasizing throughout the last three chapters. As we discuss language games you can play with your preschooler to help him develop these preliteracy skills, you want to repeatedly and frequently model the language concept you are showing your preschooler. Only after that might you occasionally ask your preschooler to demonstrate what he is learning. Keep in mind, for all of the suggestions below, the idea is to provide lots of rich learning experiences with your preschooler, not to "train" him to be a reader or writer. Remember, your role is to be a supportive parent who interacts, not interrogates.

Ideas for Around the House

Pretty much anything you do, in any place within the house, can be a literacy learning experience for you and your preschooler. Whether during more formal literacy situations, like reading to your child, or in less formal situations, such as making meals or doing chores, you can provide activities and experiences that will prove to be beneficial to your preschooler.

Reading Time

Undoubtedly, you've already realized the importance of reading to your preschooler. Reading to your preschooler will help develop both her spoken and written language skills. As we have mentioned before, reading can expand her vocabulary and enable her to learn different ways of saying the same thing.

While all children's books are useful for helping your preschooler learn about spoken and written language, you may wish to think about more than the topic of the books as you read to your preschooler. For example, find some books that involve rhyming (titles by Dr. Seuss and Shel Silverstein or any book that emphasizes rhyming). By reading these books repeatedly to your preschooler, chances are she will catch on and begin to provide rhyming words before you can turn the page. Thus, reading these types of books to your preschooler helps her to focus on the sounds of our language without requiring her to sit through a lesson on rhyming.

Find some books that involve rhyming. Reading these types of books to your preschooler helps her to focus on the sounds of our language without requiring her to sit through a lesson on rhyming.

You also might try and group together other books for reading that seem to contain simple plots involving problems, actions, and solutions. Many children's books will follow this format, perhaps with more than one problem-action-solution sequence. As you read and reread these books to your preschooler, engage her in the book-reading activity by pausing at logical points in the story and talking about what she and you think might happen next. This can help her to develop and use her understanding of cause and effect to predict or infer the plot of a story. If possible or appropriate, relate the story line to her own life. For example, you might engage her in a conversation about her experiences with the topic of the book, or, after finishing the book, make up a new story that inserts her as the main character. These types of activities serve to increase her understanding of storytelling and help her prepare for the day when she begins to read books on her own and must "read between the lines" to help make sense of the information.

As you read to your four- and five-year-old preschooler, you also can begin to draw attention to the print on the paper and the speech sounds of our language. For example, as you read, you might, at logical stopping points, comment on how the character's name begins with the same sound as her name ("Kitty. . . . That has a *k* sound, just like your name . . . Caitlin. Hmmm . . . ? We use a *k* or a *c* to write the *k* sound.").

After finishing the book, you can review it, showing and then asking your preschooler about words that begin with certain letters, or words that seem exceptionally long. You also may find yourself occasionally drawing your finger across the sentence as you read to her. As you do this, you might time your pointing with the words you read, so that it becomes clearer where words begin and end. These different types of interactions help increase your preschooler's knowledge of sounds, print, and words.

Mealtime

Most families, no matter how busy, inevitably end up being together for mealtimes. Though these times can be hectic amid the bustle of preparing dinner and talking about everyone's day, they also can be used as means for facilitating your preschooler's understanding of written language. For example, when the family is sitting down for breakfast, you can use the milk carton and some cereal as a way to develop knowledge of sounds, words, and print. Consider the following scenario:

Father: "Look at this word *milk*. It sure is a small word. Let's see how many letters are in that word."

Child: (Father and child pointing to letters) "1, 2, 3, 4. Four."

Father: "Right! And it is short to say. *Milk* (clap). But look how much milk there is (holding up carton). Even though there is lots of milk, it has a short name. Now, look at this word *Cheerios*. Let's count the letters in this word."

Child: "1, 2, 3, 4, 5, 6, 7, 8. Eight letters."

Father: "Wow! Eight letters. And it takes a long time to say: *Cheer* (clap), *ri* (clap), *os* (clap). Three claps. But look at this tiny Cheerio. It's so small. Even though it has a long name, it is so tiny!"

Simple discussions, such as this one about the length of words, help preschoolers understand that words are not part of the objects they name. This increases their metalinguistic knowledge of print and words.

Other games you might play at mealtime include a rhyming game, thinking of all the words that rhyme with your meal (*egg, leg, beg* . . .). The family can pick a letter of the day and see who can find the most occurrences of that letter on the bread bag. The ideas are endless. The point here is not to turn every mealtime into a quiz or lesson on words, sounds, and letters. Rather, it is to emphasize that a minute here or a minute there directed toward what you know about written language can lead to great payoffs in your preschooler's literacy development.

Chore Time

Even though we typically consider chores around the house as more of a burden than a pleasure, we actually can take advantage of those times to provide learning experiences for our children. For example, as you help your preschooler put away her toys, you can arrange the toys on the shelf by the length of the sound of their name, rather than by size. As you wash the dishes, you can clap out the number of syllables you hear in the dishes and utensils you put in the dishwasher—"Knife (clap), spatula (clap,

clap, clap)." As you carry the laundry downstairs, use each step to say one word of a sentence—"We (step), are (step), almost (step), done! (step)." Your preschooler will be learning to play and talk about language, while helping you accomplish the household chores. What a bargain!

Ideas When Traveling

When we were growing up, both of us were part of families who played alphabet games in the car. These games involved finding words on street signs or billboards that began with an *a*, then a *b*, and so on through the alphabet. We played games that required us to rhyme words with objects that one of our siblings saw and called out. Unbeknownst to us, we were learning about print and the sounds letters make as we played these games. It seems that these games have gone by the wayside for many families. Even though we would like to start a movement to bring them back, these games are not the only ones that you can play with your preschooler that will help her to learn about written language. In fact, your play with words can occur without any reference to what is outside of the car. When her dad was taking Genevieve to early piano lessons, they would play a game that involved thinking of different definitions of a word. For example:

Dad: "Block. Like blocks kids play with, we live on a block, he's a blockhead."

Genevieve: "Pet. I have a pet. I pet Wendy."

Other games can be those that model and ask children to think of opposites of words (hot . . . cold) or categories of words (dogs: Lab, poodle, wiener dog . . .). These games encourage your preschooler to think about words themselves, rather than just use them in a sentence. By thinking of the word itself, she is practicing her metalinguistic skills. And as we have said, these skills provide an excellent groundwork for literacy.

Ideas When Shopping

Shopping can be a time when you just want to buy your groceries or clothes and get home, especially when your preschooler is asking for a pretzel or a quarter to ride the mini-carousel outside the store. However, you again can turn this outing into a fun-filled learning time for your preschooler. Before heading off for the store, make a list, but write the list in front of your preschooler. Talk aloud as you write the list. Your list writing might sound like the following:

"Let's see . . . we need milk."

(Write *milk*.)

"Hmm, *milk* has four letters. Now, we also need eggs."

(Write *eggs*.)

"Hey, I hear three sounds—*eh, g, z,* but I had to write four letters."

By exposing your preschooler to the way you write language on paper, and your thought processes and observations about what you write, he will be learning a great deal about print and how we produce it. In other words, he will be learning, indirectly, about spelling.

After completing your list, take it to the store and have your preschooler help you cross off the words as you put the items in your cart. As he does this, you can talk, or ask him, about the words. Your discussions might be like the following:

"Pop. That doesn't take very long to say, and the word you crossed out is pretty short, even though that's a really big bottle. And look at this. Macaroni. That's pretty long there, where I wrote it. It takes a longer time to say it, too. But these macaronis sure are small."

In these kinds of interchanges, your preschooler not only is learning how words are separate from the objects they identify, he also is learning about the purpose of writing: to inform, to remind, and so on. These simple examples demonstrate that children can learn about language even during the most common, everyday activities.

Chapter Summary

OBVIOUSLY, THE IDEAS we provide in these different situations are interchangeable (you can play rhyming games during shopping trips or make lists of chores to do around the house). The point is to show how you don't need to buy fancy toys or products to help your preschooler learn to read and write. You have the materials and know-how to do this right now in your home or car. Take advantage of these opportunities. Lay the foundation that will help develop the knowledge and skills she will need to tackle that most difficult of school tasks: reading and writing.

5

The Influence of Gender and Birth Order on Language Development

DID YOU KNOW?

- Parents talk differently to girls than they do to boys.
- Younger children actually learn valuable language skills when they are around their older siblings.
- "Twin talk" is somewhat of a myth.

The young parents were excited. Their second child, a daughter, had been born. They felt they knew what to expect: feeding, bathing, diapering, clothing, diapering, and feeding again. This would be second nature to them. But the one factor that was new was that this second child created a sibling for their three-year-old son. How would he react? Had they prepared him enough? They had talked with him many times about the new baby coming into his life. He had been prepped on what it was like to hear crying at odd hours of the day and night. They had even "borrowed" a friend's baby for an afternoon, so he could see what it was like to have an infant around the house. Now, today was the big day. He was meeting his little sister for the first time. He entered the birth room with his father. There, on his mother's lap was his new sister. He gazed on her, looked up at his parents and then said, "She's not talking!" Apparently, they had forgotten one little detail!

Just like other parents, we were somewhat apprehensive when each of our children was born. With our firstborn child, we wondered if we had the type of parenting skills and instincts that would help our baby grow physically and mentally. With the arrival of our second-born child, we wondered how the older child would handle the presence of the younger child. Just like you are doing now, we read what we could on how parents and siblings affect the growth and development of children. We found some fascinating information, including how gender, birth order, and siblings affect language development. In this chapter, we share that information with you. Before we begin, though, we have two points to make.

> All children are unique—just when you think you know everything, a child will throw you for a loop!

As you read this chapter, it will be important for you to remember that the information we report on the effects of gender, birth order, and siblings on language development is what researchers have found *in general.* While studies suggest that girls generally acquire certain words before boys and firstborns typically use a certain style of language, these findings are not definite in every situation. Thus, it is very likely, as you will see from some of our examples with our own children, that your child may not follow the patterns or strategies of language for his gender or birth order we describe. This should not be a cause for concern. All children are unique, and one thing we have learned in our professional and parental experiences, just when you think you know everything, a child will throw you for a loop! Use this information to gain a deeper understanding of how the intriguing process of language acquisition *can* occur. We think that the more you read about the process of language development, the more fascinated and impressed you will become with what your child is learning and *how* he is doing it.

Our second point is to remind you of something you read in chapter 2. As you recall, we talked about how children may approach early language development using different "styles." The baby with a *referential* style approaches learning language by focusing more on nouns and playing naming games. A baby with an *expressive* style likes to play social-interaction games and uses many more words that describe actions or serve to help the baby interact *(please, more, allgone)*. We bring these styles up again now because these styles of language development are often associated with children of a specific gender or birth order, though not 100 percent of the time by any means. Nevertheless, it is helpful to keep in mind these styles and what they mean as you read the rest of this chapter.

Language is one of the most crucial areas of development in a child's life. The fact that gender, birth order, and siblings may influence it is worthy of note. We have said all along that you are one of the most important aspects of your child's language development. This chapter should help you understand this fact even more, while helping you to learn how certain biological and familial factors also influence your child's language development. Let's get started.

Gender Effects on Language Development

PERHAPS ONE OF the most frequently asked questions we receive when we lecture on language development is: Do girls and boys develop language differently? The answer is both yes and no. There *are* some differences in how many, but not all, boys approach language learning when they are compared to many, but not all, girls. However, when you look at the greater picture (that is, the complete development of language), there are many more similarities than differences. Both genders acquire language skills along the same timeline. Both become active, engaging conversationalists. True, there may be some differences in interactional styles when you compare adult men and women (after all, they *are* from different planets!); however, the difference between the sexes during the first five years of life is not vast.

Differences Between Girls and Boys

Researchers have attempted to find differences between girls and boys by administering formal language tests and determining whether the two sexes differ in their scores. In some studies, girls have performed better on tests that focus on expressive language, or how advanced they are in what they can say. However, other studies have not found similar results. For the most part, research that has examined whether boys and girls understand language differently has consistently yielded no differences. Thus, on very general measures of language skills, there appear to be no differences between boys' and girls' language skills. However, other studies that have focused on specific skills have found some slight differences.

During the first few years of life, differences between boys and girls may be apparent when their word meanings are examined. For example, research has shown that girls are more likely to begin using emotion words (words such as *love, like, sad, happy*) before boys do. Obviously, boys are not considered to be delayed in their use of these words, and ultimately they do use them. However, there may be a time delay between when girls begin using these words and boys first say them.

Girls are typically first to use language to collaborate with their peers to solve problems during play situations. When confronted with a situation that requires some strategy as a means of solving a problem, preschool girls are more likely to talk about possible solutions with one another. They may initiate more turns in a conversation about the problem and ask for help more frequently. They also tend to describe how they solved a problem as they accomplish the task. On the other hand, preschool boys are more likely to attempt to work through problems with actions. Over time, boys also begin problem solving by talking with their peers. Even though there are initial differences in how the two genders try to solve problems (using language versus acting on the problem), their successes in solving problems are similar.

One additional potential difference between boys and girls is the style of language development they tend to use. Studies have shown that approximately 78 percent of all girls have a referential style of language acquisition, while approximately 60 percent of all boys have an expressive style. Thus, girls are likely to use more nouns than boys, show a preference for naming games, and demonstrate clearer speech than boys.

Possible Causes for Gender Effects on Language Development

What might lead to these subtle differences in the language development of boys and girls? Not surprisingly, it appears, at least in part, to come back to . . . YOU! When researchers have studied parents (mostly moms) interacting with their two- or three-year-old children, they have observed that parents use different types of language with boys than with girls.

Mothers of two-year-olds tend to ask more open-ended questions of their daughters, use more child-directed speech (see chapter 2 for our discussion of child-directed speech), and produce longer and more complex sentences than they do with their sons. They also just talk more to girls than they do to boys. When mothers are talking to their two-year-old sons, they use language more to direct their sons than they do with their daughters. They also may be less articulate than they are with their daughters.

The differences in parent-talk aimed at boys and girls also extend to the specific situations where language is used. In a number of studies, researchers have examined where parents are more likely to initiate or begin conversations with their children. In studies of parents and their three-year-old children, research has shown that parents are most likely to initiate conversation with their boys in play situations than in other situations. However, with their daughters, they are more likely to initiate conversations during "nonplay" times and in situations that require help.

How do these research findings about parent-child interactions tie into the subtle differences between boys and girls? When parents initiate conversation more to their boys in play situations, they likely are talking about what is occurring at that moment in time. Thus, their language will naturally be less complex and less abstract than if they were talking about topics out of their sons' present surroundings. Chances are, their language is about the actions occurring rather than on naming of objects. Parents also may not feel compelled to be particularly articulate in these types of informal situations. This may explain why boys develop the use of language to talk about emotions and to solve problems later than girls. These types of language skills and meanings just may not occur as much in these parent-child interactions. It also suggests that parents are matching their sons' style of acquisition, focusing more on interactions and less on naming.

However, when parents initiate more language during nonplay times with their daughters, they likely are using more complex and lengthier sentences to talk about situations and events out of the present, including talking about feelings. By asking questions of their daughters, they also may be modeling how we use language to solve problems as well as focusing on labeling of objects or people. This latter interaction would match many daughters' preferences for nouns. Thus, the way parents interact with their children, and when they choose to do this the most, may occur because parents are matching their children's style preferences. This, in turn, may set the stage for when girls and boys acquire certain language skills.

Finally, one cannot overlook the actual play activities of boys and girls as an additional explanation for why there might be subtle differences between the sexes in language development. When children are playing with dolls, there is a greater chance that the language used during that play will involve more nouns and more questions. When children are engaged in play with vehicles, there is a greater chance that creative sounds or noises will be used and less actual real words will be produced.

Now, we don't want to suggest that play with dolls is "girl play" and that play with cars and trucks is "boy play." Indeed, for all of our children, we made all types of toys available. However, there does seem to be some relationship between dolls and girls and cars and boys. Perhaps children are biased by parents who purchase their toys, by the media that promotes certain stereotypes, or even by some basic biological differences. Nevertheless, boys *tend* to play more with trucks and cars, and girls *tend* to play more with dolls. Thus, the actual play situations may also influence their language development. Whether the play influences the style of language the child uses, or the style of language influences the play is unknown.

An experience from a holiday gift exchange several years ago illustrates the differences in boy-girl language seen in one of our households. It was a tradition to allow the children to open their presents from each other on Christmas Eve and save the rest of the gifts for the next morning. Caleb received a Godzilla action figure from his sister, and Caitlin received a Barbie doll from her brother. About an hour after the exchange, their parents walked in to quietly observe their play. At first, they were surprised to see that Caleb was playing with Barbie and Caitlin was playing with Godzilla. As they listened carefully, however, the play itself wasn't surprising after all . . .

> There are more similarities than differences in how boys and girls acquire language skills.

Caleb had Barbie by the fireplace yelling, "Get back from the building, everyone!" (sounds of screaming, gunfire, bombs exploding, and so on) "The bomb has gone off! The bomb has gone off!" (more screaming).

Godzilla, on the other hand, was over by the coffee table, saying to Baby Jesus and the rest of the characters from the manger scene, "Hi. What a nice baby! Do you need a blanket to keep you warm? Will you be my new friend?"

Summary of Gender Effects

The bottom line regarding the effect of gender on language development is that there are more similarities than differences in how boys and girls acquire their language skills. Any subtle, temporary differences may be due to how and when parents interact with their children, as well as the types of play situations in which the children engage. So, enjoy your son or daughter, expose him or her to different types of play situations, and interact with your child in a variety of situations. This will only serve to increase the experiences and language models from which your child can benefit.

Also, remember that for all of the differences we discussed, not all girls demonstrate a certain trait and not all boys use a certain language strategy. In other words, do not panic if your daughter has a "male strategy" or your son has a language skill attributed to young girls. What we want you to take from this review is simply that there are some aspects of language development that differ between some boys and girls and that, knowing this information, you may be able to spot those difference in your son or daughter. The differences will not be problems, just alternative ways of achieving the same goal: language development.

> Enjoy your daughter or son, expose him or her to different types of play situations, and interact with your child in a variety of situations.

Birth Order, Siblings, and Language Development

BOTH OF US have one son and one daughter. For each of us, our son was the firstborn and our daughter was the second-born. During the second pregnancies, we were somewhat un-certain as to how our sons would deal with the new arrivals. Because of this, we did everything possible to prepare them—Nick is Kenn's son, Caleb is Julie's son—for their new siblings. We talked about the need for Mommy and Daddy to attend more to the baby's needs at first, that there might be crying at night (and this wouldn't be just from the baby!), and so on. Nick seemed to take it all in stride. He often took interested visitors on tours of "the baby's" room. In Caleb's case, he, too, took the process seriously. He was adamant throughout the pregnancy that the new child would be a girl, even correcting the obstetrician. During ultrasounds, when the physician would point out "his" head, Caleb would butt in and say, "There's HER head!" Both of us were sure our sons were not only incredibly prepared for the new arrivals, but equally excited about the prospect of a sibling.

When the blessed days arrived, however, both boys reacted in ways that we could not have foreseen. Even though Kenn was sure he had prepared Nick for his new baby sister and that he would greet her with open arms, Nick's first comment on seeing her was, "*Now* can we go to McDonald's?!" Caleb's reaction was somewhat delayed compared to Nick's, but decidedly more straightforward. After approximately two weeks of having his baby sister in the house, he hung a picture on the door of a baby with the familiar "no" sign (circle with slash through it)

around the picture. About the same time, he said, "I know I love her, but do we have to *keep* her?" Thus, both boys' enthusiasm regarding the arrival of their new baby sisters quickly dissolved with the actual appearance of the infant.

Just as parents may not be able to completely control how their child will react to the birth of a sibling, so, too, will parents have little control over how the language environments differ between that of their firstborn and subsequent children. There has been considerable study of the language skills and the communicative environment of children who are firstborn or later-born. The findings suggest that both parents and siblings may be at the root of differences in language development based on birth order. As you will see, the manner in which parents and siblings interact with one another may be intricately tied to the situational factors that are more than likely out of a parent's control.

Differences Between Firstborn and Later-Born Children

Some studies have shown that firstborn children are more likely to have larger vocabularies during their second year of life and reach the fifty-word milestone (when most toddlers begin to use two-word sentences, the first appearance of syntax use) sooner than later-born children.

In addition, about two-thirds of firstborn children use a referential style of language acquisition, while about two-thirds of later-born children take on an expressive style of language development. Nick and Genevieve did not follow this particular scenario. Nick, the firstborn, was very much an expressive language learner. Genevieve seemed to be referential from the very beginning. Of course, it may have been, in their case, that gender "won" over birth order. However, both Caleb and Caitlin were referential. This does not fit the typical pattern in that Caleb is a male and Caitlin is second-born. Thus, as we have stated all along, research findings in these areas provide tendencies but not absolutes.

Other studies have found additional differences between siblings. Children who are later-born have been shown to develop certain conversational skills earlier than did their firstborn siblings. For example, later-born children are more likely to stay on topic by relating what they say to what others are saying. This is a particularly important conversational skill. We're sure you have been in conversations with someone where the balance of the conversation seems one-sided. The individual seems

> Firstborn children are more likely to have larger vocabularies during their second year of life than later-born children.

to talk more about what she is interested in and less about what you are discussing. None of us particularly like these types of situations, because we intuitively expect our listener to react to and expand on the topic we have begun. Thus, using contingent sentences, or relating one's sentences to others' remarks in conversations, is a crucial skill to develop, and one that later-born children seem to master sooner. Perhaps it is not surprising, then, that other studies have found that later-born children may be more successful early on in developing friendships with peers.

Possible Causes for Language Differences in Siblings

The differences noted between firstborn children and later-born children is likely due to a several factors, including the fact that no two children seem to be *exactly* the same in how they learn language. However, the differences in sibling language development are likely due to the very real differences in the language environment in which they are raised. In other words, the situation in which firstborn children are originally raised is unlike that of later-born children. These differences, then, often center on the parent and the siblings.

At least until a second child is born, a firstborn child is by definition the only child in the home. This means that, in most cases, the child has the relatively undivided attention of his mother and father. On the other hand, the second-born child has at least one more member in the household than the firstborn child had. Because of this, firstborn children *tend* to have more one-on-one parent-child time than do later-born children. Researchers have found that parents of firstborn children are more likely to use more complex sentences and ask fewer direct questions than parents who have more than one child. Parents of one child are also likely to provide more helpful support, that of child-directed speech discussed in chapter 2, than parents with more than one child. Thus, firstborn children, at least while they are the only child, are likely to receive a high degree of language models that are extremely helpful for language development.

When there is more than one child in the home, parent language interactions tend to address less of their input directly to each child. So, for example, even though with a second child parents have doubled their number of children, they do not double the amount of language they use with their children. When parents are addressing several children, they are more likely to be directive than when addressing firstborn children or an only child.

Of course, one could argue that parents do not need to double their language input when they have more than one child, because the later-born children are receiving language models from their older siblings. Researchers have been intrigued about this possibility and have studied the language input of older children to their younger siblings.

> If the older sibling is school age, then there is a good chance that he will use child-directed speech with his younger sibling.

Studies have shown that the age of the older sibling influences the quality of the language input to the younger sibling. In general, the greater the age gap between children (that is, the older the firstborn sibling is when the younger child is beginning to acquire language), the more facilitative the input to the younger child. If, for example, the older sibling is school age, then there is a good chance that he will use child-directed speech with his younger sibling. However, if the older child is a preschooler himself, the use of child-directed speech to support the language development of his younger sibling decreases dramatically. Interestingly, some child language experts have suggested that this still could be helpful for the child. It may be that the less-than-perfect input and modeling by the slightly older sibling prepares the younger sibling for talking with strangers, who by definition may not be as tuned in to the child's language level and needs.

At first, this information on siblings may make it seem as though later-born children do not experience many benefits from the language environment in which they are born. They are likely receiving less one-on-one language models than their older sibling. However, there are definite positive attributes to the language environment for later-born children to which firstborn children have much less exposure. For example, later-born children have many more early experiences with multiple-person conversations. That is, because of the presence of at least one older sibling, later-born children hear and partake in more conversations where two or more individuals are talking. This can be helpful in a number of ways.

In two-person conversations, it is fairly easy to take turns. When one person stops talking, the other can begin. In multiple-person conversations, each individual has to negotiate her turn to speak. Being part of a multiple-person conversation means each person must pay close attention to the others' signals as to when they are finished with their thought or when they want to jump into the conversation. These signals involve changes in the rate or melody of their voice, the language they are using (such as a question), and their body language, such as hand gestures, eye contact, and so forth.

As a mature language user, you have come to understand the signals for when you can talk in a multiple-person conversation. Because later-born children are part of multiple-person conversations, they must quickly learn these signals as well. Research has shown that later-born children acquire these conversational skills earlier than do their older siblings.

We should warn you that the rules for negotiating multiple-speaker turns become inordinately more complex during car trips and when parents are on the phone. Those two situations seem to have a mysterious influence on your children's desire to tell you something right then! We ultimately resorted at times to very explicit strategies for car talk: "Nick may say two things. Okay, now it's Genevieve's turn. You can say your two things." Occasionally, Kenn was also given a turn to talk.

Being part of multiple-person conversations also has other advantages. In multiple-person conversations, there are many more chances for children to hear pronouns (such as *she, he, him, her*) being used. This may seem odd, but it makes sense when you consider the circumstances. In one-on-one parent-child interactions, parents are more likely to talk about the "here-and-now." Thus, much of the talk will be focused on the child and what he is doing. Also, parents are more likely to refer to themselves by their label, Mommy or Daddy, in these situations ("Give it to Mommy."). However, in multiple-person conversations, the extra individuals lead to an increase in the use of pronouns. Parents also tend to use more pronouns for themselves ("Give it to me.") than in one-on-one situations.

Research has shown that later-born children acquire certain conversational skills earlier than do their older siblings.

Not surprisingly, then, later-born children learn to use pronouns earlier than their older siblings. This may seem trivial, but understanding and using pronouns is not an easy task for children. Thus, being a later-born child definitely is a plus in this area of language development.

Finally, even though parents are not talking more when they have more than one child, the conversations they have with their children may be longer in length. This may be an advantage for the later-born children. Learning about language in conversations with multiple-persons is not an easy task, as we stated above. With longer episodes of multiple-person conversations, later-born children in essence have longer "lessons" or models from which to develop their understanding of how to use language with others.

The Special Circumstance of Multiple Births

Some children fit into both categories: first-born and born into a sibling situation. This occurs, of course, when a child is part of a multiple birth. Because most of the research on multiple births has focused on twins, the information we present is largely based on these studies. However, with the increase in larger multiple births, and the slowly increasing number of research studies conducted with them, we expect to know more about language development and larger groups of children, such as triplets, quadruplets, and quintuplets. Until then, the limited information on larger multiple births suggest that the information we relay below holds true for them as well, with the possible exception that larger multiple-birth situations put children more at risk for language delays.

Initially, twins may lag behind single-birth children in their language development. Part of this could be due to biological or medical reasons, such as premature birth. With some premature births, accompanying medical complications may interfere with a child's development in many areas, including language. In cases of premature birth for any child, it is wise to determine whether she is reaching her language milestones based on calculating her age from her full-term due date, rather than her actual birth date. By compensating in this way, what may appear to be a delay will not be.

Nevertheless, there is some research that suggests that twins may lag behind single-birth children even when compensations are taken into account. Twins have been shown to have smaller vocabularies during the second year of life and demonstrate less joint attention with their mothers. Others have delays in other areas, such as their speech development and grammar.

Some language specialists have suggested these possible delays occur because twins are sufficient company for one another and adult interaction is not needed. While this may seem obvious, other studies have found that most twins prefer to interact with their parents rather than with the other child. Some experts have suggested that possible delays are due to the lack of one-on-one situations. By definition, twins do not have the same experience with parents that only or firstborn children have. However, as we discussed, this is not necessarily a disadvantage, especially when one considers the multiple-person conversational skills that twins learn early on. Thus, just as later-born children have advantages in language environment compared to firstborn children, so, too, do children from multiple births.

It is not uncommon to hear people talk about "twin talk." Twin talk has become somewhat of an urban legend. With twin talk, twins are reportedly speaking a new and self-created language with one another, a language that no other individual understands. As you might imagine, this has definitely peaked the interest of language researchers. What they have found has considerably put into question the existence of twin talk, at least as described by popular media.

> With twin talk, twins are reportedly speaking a new and self-created language with one another, a language that no other individual understands.

Researchers have studied twins who reportedly use twin talk. Specifically, they have examined how the siblings interact with one another and the actual speech sounds they use. They have found that twins are more likely than single-born children to imitate and respond to the vocal play (nonlanguage sounds, such as babbling and other creative noises) their sibling is using. Through imitation and repetition of vocal play, each twin is learning how to produce sounds like her twin, while simultaneously learning to make speech sounds like her parents. The result may be an initial different knowledge of speech sounds. In fact, twins who have been thought to be using twin talk have been found to have delayed speech development. This is not to say that all twins develop speech and language delays. However, what it does suggest is that few if any sets of multiple-birth siblings are creating a language known only to them.

Summary of Birth Order Differences

Even though there are some noticeable differences between firstborn and later-born children, it is important to realize that these differences do not lead to greater likelihood of language problems. There is no research to suggest that birth order is tied to language learning problems. Indeed, as we mentioned in our discussion of gender effects on language development, there are more similarities than differences in language acquisition among siblings.

We frequently hear that a younger sibling is not talking because his older siblings talk for him. Indeed, this *could* be the case. However, just because older siblings talk for a younger one, does not mean one should not expect the younger child to talk. Our advice for this particular situation is to not assume that a child who is not talking, or who is delayed in his language skills, *could* talk if his siblings didn't talk for him. Instead, if a child is not using the language skills we outlined in chapters 1 to 4 when he should be, parents should seek professional advice. We talk about how to do this in chapter 9.

Chapter Summary

IN OUR PERSONAL lives, we are experiencing what it is like to parent sons and daughters, firstborn children and second-born children. We have seen in both our personal and professional lives how gender and birth order can influence language development in different yet exciting ways. We hope that this chapter has provided some answers to questions you had about the effects of gender and birth order on language acquisition. We hope that, as we did, you find these differences both fascinating and worthy of observation.

Gender, birth order, and siblings are not the only influences that can impact language development. Other family variables, such as language, dialect, and culture may influence language development as well. Our next chapter adds to your growing body of knowledge by explaining how your language, your culture, and your thoughts on the importance of these factors can affect how your child learns language.

6

The Influence of Culture on Language

DID YOU KNOW?

- Most children can learn two languages in the same amount of time it takes adults to learn one language.
- Children learning two languages at once benefit when the languages are spoken by different adults.
- Everyone has a dialect.

John and Maria are the proud parents of a 13-month-old girl. Even though little Grace is beginning to use some words, her parents are nervous about her speech and language development. When speaking to Grace, John uses English. On the other hand, Maria, whose native language is Spanish, has been speaking Spanish to Grace since birth. However, both parents are now worried that they might be confusing their daughter, setting her up for a difficult time in learning language. They wonder if they are "harming" their daughter's chances of speaking Standard American English (SAE) and setting her up for difficulties in school and possible ridicule. They've gone to a speech-language pathologist to ask how they can "talk better" to their child.

John and Maria's concerns are not unique. In chapters 1 to 4, we presented a review of how children develop speech and language during the first five years of life, based on research conducted mainly with children in the United States. Unlike what one might assume, however, these children were learning variations of SAE. Some children were learning speech and language influenced by the regional variations of English used where they live (for example, Southern English, African-American English, Middle Atlantic English), while others were learning English in addition, or secondary, to another language. In fact, children in the United States do not learn a strict, "pure" version of English. Rather, all children are learning a variation of SAE. Thus, instead of feeling that their situation is rare, John and Maria will come to realize that they are much more typical than they thought.

In this chapter, we provide information about the variations that may occur in language development because of cultural, geographical, and family influences, as well as about the purpose for which language is used. This discussion includes how language acquisition differs because of additional languages being learned or dialects in the parents' speech. We also talk about the benefits of bilingual development as well as fears parents often express when raising their children bilingually. We include in this chapter important factors to consider when raising your child in a bilingual or bidialectal home. The topic of this chapter is not only an important one for you and your young, developing child, it is also a serious social topic as well. As you will see, we will try to disperse the common myths and prejudices some individuals hold when they encounter others who speak somewhat differently than they do.

Cultural and Linguistic Variations in Language Acquisition

WHEN YOU WERE growing up, you probably encountered other children and their parents who communicated some-what differently than you did. It may have been that these were families whose first language was not English. These families were speaking English, albeit a variation of the English you spoke. Others may have been families who had moved from another part of the country and brought with them the sounds and vocabulary specific to that region. We are betting that after a few days of attending to the differences between their speech and language and yours, you stopped noticing the variations. This is exactly what happens to most people. Awareness of variations in the way speech is produced or language is used quickly fades when a communication partner decides to listen for meaning rather than differences. Nevertheless, it is helpful to review what the effects are of growing up in a home where the English language is not the main language, or the only lan-guage, being learned. It is also important to talk about what differences in dialects might mean. This discussion should help us be better informed about the wide range of typical varia-tions in our English language as well as dispel myths about these variations.

Growing Up with Two or More Languages

John and Maria's concerns for Grace are those often held by many parents of children who are learning English as a second language to the primary language in the home. Children may learn to speak English either simultaneously or sequentially. Simultaneous language development is when a child is learning more than one language at a time, as was the case with Grace. Sequential language development is when a child learns

one language initially and then at a later date learns a second language. This may occur during the early years (three to five years) when the child is still learning the first language, or it may occur when she attends formal school, after she has acquired a great deal of the first language. In either case, it is important to know how best to expose the child to the second language.

Simultaneous Bilingual Development

A great deal is known about children who are learning more than one language at a time. Studies have shown that as children learn two or more languages, there is a good chance that they may use one word in one language and another word in another language. That is, children are exposed to different languages and usually those languages are attached to different people and purposes. So, children learn the words that are used for those interactions that may be different. For example, the words used at home in French may be different from the words used in the Italian-speaking day care center. So, the child might know the words for ham and eggs in French because that is what her mother prepares, but will know the word for paint or clay in Italian because those are materials used in the day care center. Initially, children may use words from the two different languages in one phrase or sentence when they are communicating, although they may also use only words from the language that their communication partner knows. This latter situation may occur when it is very clear to the child what particular language a specific individual speaks. For example, it may be that Grace would use English when speaking to her father and Spanish when conversing with her mother.

Although children may initially blend the sounds from each language as they start to talk, they quickly learn to differentiate which sounds go with which language. Granted, many sounds may be shared by both languages. However, there will be some speech sounds that are used in one language and not the other. In these cases, children by the age of three are usually differentiating the speech sounds of each language.

As children develop further, they learn to recognize how two words, spoken differently in each language, have the same meaning. They begin demonstrating the ability to relate a word in one language (*dog*) to the corresponding word in the second language (*perro*). When Caleb was two, he had a wonderful nanny, Celia, who spoke only Spanish and lived in the family home. Celia stayed with the family until Caleb was five years old. During that time, he acquired both Spanish and English, as Caleb's parents asked the nanny to speak only Spanish to him. His appreciation for the difference in word use in the two languages was demonstrated one afternoon when he was almost three years old. He was walking by a large fountain and he pointed and said *water*. He then followed that comment with, "Celia say *agua*." This statement not only illustrated Caleb's appreciation for the notion of distinct languages, but also his knowledge that words actually stand for objects, an early metalinguistic skill (see chapter 4).

While this ability to recognize the similarities and differences in words and how they sound develops relatively early on, children will likely need more time to learn the more complex differences, such as the syntax, or word order, of the two languages. At first, children learn simple sentence structures in both languages ("I like ice cream."), but as they begin to tackle more complex syntax, children will likely learn how to say longer and trickier sentences in one language before the other.

Generally, between the ages of five and seven, a child learning two languages simultaneously will have mastered both languages, understanding and using the different words, speech sounds, and sentence types of each language. This assumes, of course, that the child has been exposed to both languages equally and had comparable experiences in both. There may be some continued blending of the two languages when he speaks, but this is likely to occur when he is uncertain about a word in one language and uses a more familiar word in the other language to complete his thought, just as many adults do. In fact, after five years of age, children may mix a word from one language into another because that is what they have observed adults to do. This ability to mix words for different purposes and situations is actually considered a high-level linguistic skill.

> Generally, between the ages of five and seven, a child learning two languages simultaneously will have mastered both languages.

As a child is learning two languages simultaneously, it will be helpful for the parents to expose the child to the different languages by using each language in its own separate context. For example, the situation in which little Grace was learning Spanish and English was ideal. In her case, her father was speaking to her in English and her mother was speaking to her in Spanish. This is what happened with Caleb. His nanny, Celia, spoke only Spanish to him, while his parents spoke only English. Other parents may set up situations where one language is spoken in one situation (for example, Spanish is spoken by both parents when they are at Grandma's house) and the other language is spoken in another situation (English is spoken in the home). By separating the languages into clear-cut situations or with specific individuals, the learning of that language is considered easier because it gives the child the opportunity to experience each language system separately and completely.

Children learning two languages simultaneously will become successful communicators in each language in about the same amount of time as children learning only one language. Thus, although some parents fear that bilingual language learning can cause a slow rate of development, children are adept at learning two (or more) languages without any difficulties or lingering inefficiencies. In fact, children who are multiple-language learners may have several advantages over monolingually developing children. Some studies suggest that children learning more than one language may perform higher on formal vocabulary tests and develop some metalinguistic skills earlier than their monolingual peers. As the country becomes more and more multilingual, individuals who can speak more than one language will have expanded opportunities to communicate with many more individuals and likely understand other people's points of view in more empathetic ways.

Sequential Bilingual Development

In other situations, children learn to speak one language at home and then must learn a second language in a childcare situation or at school. When children begin learning a second language after the age of three, they are considered to be learning the two languages sequentially. How children learn the second language, and the manner in which the first language is respected, may determine how well both languages are learned, used, and maintained.

Some children may learn a second language mainly through social interactions with peers who speak that second language. In these cases, a monolingual child typically begins to learn a second language by developing social connections with her peers and relying on standard words or phrases to interact with these friends. She may quickly learn to say *okay, I don't know,* and other key phrases to simulate adequate language use in the second language and give the appearance of being engaged in the conversation. In these initial language-learning situations, some children will actively try new words and phrases in the second language, supplementing these language attempts with other means of communication (gestures, facial expressions, and so on) to get their meaning across. Other children may be more hesitant to jump right in, preferring to listen and learn the language before being too active in conversations. In either case, the children are carefully listening to what their peers say, analyzing the play situations, and searching for commonly used words and phrases that seem to relate to what is being done at the moment.

After some time, children will decide to communicate with their peers in the new language, regardless of their level of capabilities. The urge to socialize through language becomes too strong to not communicate. We love that finding! It fits with our theme for this entire book—the bottom line is that language is a tool for interaction! When children reach this point, it may be that, due to their level of competence, they produce language that is a blend of the two languages. This blended language may contain words and sentence structures from both languages as well as some language invented by the child herself. This is a time when the child's capabilities may seem to change daily, as she struggles to meet the demands of communication with a level of competency that remains somewhat limited.

> The urge to socialize through language becomes too strong to not communicate.

Finally, children begin to pay more attention to the language being learned and the importance of following the rules of the new language. This may occur because, as a second language-learner slightly older than the child who learned two languages simultaneously, this learner has the ability to *think* about language. In other words, the child can use her metalinguistic skills to analyze what the rules are for the second language and take a more direct role in learning the new language.

This type of sequential language development occurs when no active or direct adult attention is given to helping the child learn the second language. In cases where a child is learning a second language in a more formal situation (that is, in a school classroom) the same type of development may or may not occur. Often, when children are required to learn a new language in a formal classroom environment, their feelings about the individuals who speak that language and their desire to communicate with them may affect how well the children learn the new language. Likewise, if the adult providing the more formal "language instruction" matches the learning style of the children, better language development should occur. For example, if a child is ready for direct instruction in language development because she has the metalinguistic skills to understand discussions *about* language, language development may be successful.

One cautionary note is important here. Even in cases where children are more aware of language and thus open to a more direct, formal approach to learning a second language, it may be that the language learned initially does not immediately prepare them for complex language situations like the classroom. This is because the language used in the classroom does not have all the extra cues (facial expressions, gestures toward the conversational topic, familiar vocabulary) that are present in regular conversational situations. Thus, the use and understanding of a second language to converse with peers does not immediately guarantee that a child will follow the language used by teachers in classrooms when they are instructing children in their lessons. It may take up to seven additional years to become proficient enough to use and comprehend the complex language used in classrooms.

Sequential language development, whether it is acquired through formal or informal means, may be affected by a number of factors. First, the age of the child when she is learning the second language can affect how well it is learned. Studies suggest that children who learn a second language after their early teen years are less likely to acquire "nativelike" speech patterns in the second language (that is, with pronunciation and intonation similar to the native language). Preteen children are more apt to acquire both languages completely. However, other factors may have a stronger effect on bilingual language development than age, including motivation, perceived need to use the language, the use of the language by siblings at home, the parents' social mobility, political agendas in the community, and so forth.

The timing in which a second language is introduced relative to the first language may affect development in both languages. If a child is *formally* taught a second language after the first language has begun to be learned but before it is completely learned, the result may be an impact on the development and use of the first language. However, as we mentioned above, if a child is more mature in her first language and has the metalinguistic skills to think about the second language, the second language may be acquired more easily without any delay in the first language.

One final factor that can affect sequential bilingual development is the amount of respect or importance attributed to each language. Unfortunately, some children may be placed in second language-learning experiences where the first language is devalued in comparison to the new language being learned. In cases such as this, it is possible that the child will decrease her use of the first language, resulting not only in a loss of skills within that first language, but also in a loss or lack of appreciation for the cultural and familial aspects of that first language. This is unfortunate because the first language typically represents the traditions and customs of the family. To diminish the importance of the home language is to devalue the importance of the family and its culture. This indeed would be a terrible mistake.

Bilingual Language Development: What Should Parents Do?

As you can see from this review of bilingual language development, children are incredibly good language learners, and not just with one language. You may be considering whether your child should learn more than one language. As you consider this possibility, keep in mind several key points. First, if you choose to provide a simultaneous, bilingual language-learning environment for your child, determine who will speak one language and who will speak the other. If one parent is speaking both languages, it is better to keep the boundaries clear, always using complete expressions in one language without mixing both languages in one sentence or thought. Remember, the clearer the boundaries between the two languages, the easier the learning. For example, Caleb expected to use Spanish with Celia and English with his mom and dad. He kept these "language boundaries" quite distinct for about two years. Then, much to the dismay of his mom, this began to change. Even though Celia never spoke English directly to Caleb, he seemed to realize that her English skills were improving because he heard her

> Children are incredibly good language learners, and not just with one language.

conversing with others in English. Gradually, he began speaking English more frequently to Celia. Interestingly, the style of English he used with Celia was different from the English used with others. When he spoke to Celia, he used many of the grammatical and phonological variations that Celia used as a native Spanish-speaker acquiring English as a second language. At the same time, his language use was characterized by the use of a variety of English typical of persons living in Mississippi, as he and his family were living in Mississippi at the time. As you might imagine, he was certainly an interesting little "case study" and many of his mom's graduate students used him as a research project!

You may wish to take a different route for your child and expose him to a second language *after* he has already learned much of his first language (after three years of age). If so, consider the information we have provided in regard to how your child will learn that second language. If you intend to expose him to the second language through interactions with his preschool peers, then let him learn through his social interactions with these friends and don't feel you have to *teach* him the language for him to be a successful communicator and play partner.

However, if your child will be learning a second language in a more formal situation that involves active teaching of the language, investigate the instructors and their method of teaching. For preschool children, you should determine whether the instructors allow the children to learn the language through "hands-on" activities, with little specific drilling of language rules. For older children, you should determine whether the instructors encourage the children to use their metalinguistic skills to help them learn new rules in the second language. Finally, regardless of age, you will want to determine whether the instructors encourage the children to maintain and respect their first language as they go about the task of acquiring the second one. If the scenarios just discussed appear to be the case, then chances are good that you have selected an appropriate language-learning environment for your child.

Learning more than one language will not put your child at risk for language-learning problems. As long as your child has ample time exposure to the languages (20-plus hours per week per language) and you use those good parenting language skills we covered in chapters 1 to 4, there is no reason to expect anything but good language development from your bilingually developing child.

Variations in Dialect

WE HAVE REVIEWED what is known about bilingual language development and provided you with some examples of what you can do to help your child learn more than one language in an efficient and worthwhile manner. As you undoubtedly know from your own experiences, another possible variation in language development has to do with the dialect(s) a child hears and uses in her speech and language.

When people consider the language used in America, many think of Standard American English (SAE). However, SAE is rarely used by individuals when speaking. In fact, the most common place one finds SAE is in written language (such as newspapers, books, and so on) and in televised newscasts (but even this seems to be decreasing). In reality, American English is represented by many different dialects. A dialect is a manner of speaking that is used by a specific group or population. Dialects are variations in speech sounds, words, word endings, sentences, and word use within a language that occur due to a number of different variables, including geographic region (for example, New England English), culture (African-American English), and learning English as a second language (Spanish-influenced English where the first language is influencing the use of English). Most dialects have evolved over time, influenced by different languages used in a particular region or culture and a historical "massaging" of the language used. Unfortunately, a lack of knowledge of the manner in which various dialects emerge has led to misconceptions of and biases against speakers of certain dialects.

Dialect Misconceptions

Some individuals assume that if a person belongs to a certain ethnic or cultural group, then that person will use characteristics of the dialect typically associated with that group. For example, it may be that when an African-American who speaks African-American English encounters another African-American, the assumption is that they share a common dialect. Of course, this may or may not be true. In this case, the dialects spoken by African-Americans will be influenced by their culture, the region of the country they are from, and others with whom they have come in contact. African-Americans from the southern states of the United States will sound differently from those in the northeast. Thus, there are likely to be differences in the dialect spoken by members of the same race.

Conversely, it may be that when some individuals hear a person using a certain dialect, they assume that person is from a certain cultural background. In fact, the person may be from a specific region of the United States that contains a large population from a specific culture. An example of this may be when an individual who has grown up in New York City is assumed to be Jewish because of the Yiddish influences on the

New York City dialect. In either case, the assumptions can lead to errors in judgment and communication.

Another misconception about dialects is that certain dialects always reflect that the speaker is using English as the second language. For example, when individuals hear others using Spanish-influenced English, they may assume that this particular dialect reflects the effects of the user's first language (Spanish) on the second language (English). While this may be the case, the dialect may also be due to home environment and culture. That is, children growing up in communities in Texas, for example, may be acquiring a variation that reflects the amalgamation of English and Spanish that has been happening for generations.

Finally, perhaps the most common and damaging misconception about certain dialects is that they do not represent accurate or "proper" English. Some individuals view certain regional dialects as inappropriate and lacking the rules of SAE. For example, the use of multiple "helping verbs" used by some individuals who speak Southern English (such as "I might could go.") is thought to be improper grammar. One of us must confess that she did not know that the grammar of SAE prohibited such combinations until she was in her doctoral program! It was used all the time in her hometown in Arkansas. In fact, the grammatical rule was covered in one of her doctoral seminars and she protested that the professor was mistaken! She explained to the professor and the other students that she used that series of words all that time ("I might could do that report. I might could have that finished by March."). They replied, "We know you do . . . !"

Others may view certain dialectal rules of African-American English as incomplete SAE, such as when an African-American speaker says, "She got five dog." What is missing in this assumption is an understanding of the rules underlying these dialects. Dialects represent differences, not errors, and they have very specific rules for the sounds, words, word endings, word use, and sentence structures to be used. Without an understanding of the notion that the English language is made up of *many* different variations, prejudices or biases may be formed.

Dialect Biases

Unfortunately, when you think about some of the dialects just discussed, as well as others found within the United States, you probably can recall a joke or two that use particular dialects to make fun of speakers of those dialects. Why does this occur? To be blunt, it often arises out of ignorance and intolerance. It seems some individuals have a difficult time accepting speech and language that differ from their own. They assume that others are not speaking "proper English" when, in fact, the same can be said about their own dialect as well. Other than what might appear in print, proper English is a rare entity, one that some may strive for, but few achieve, simply because of the regional or cultural dialects people bring to the task of talking.

> It seems some individuals have a difficult time accepting speech and language that differ from their own.

When individuals choose to make fun of dialects or those who use them, they are, in essence, making fun of cultures, families, and traditions. While some may think such jokes are harmless, one has to question the effects of these jokes on the young children who are using the dialects as part of their language. Language is an integral part of one's self-image. Hearing jokes or puns aimed at belittling certain dialects can lead to decreased self-image and self-esteem for young children. As we have said throughout this book, language is part of the individual. In this case, then, dialect also is an integral part of the individual.

Dialectal Variations in Language: What Should Parents Do?

Some parents may wonder whether the dialects they "pass on" to their children will affect their language development or, during the school years, their academic achievements. For example, we have had parents ask whether their children's dialects will affect their ability to read or spell correctly. Will their children be able to read or spell words that are said differently in their dialect? Our answer is always the same: Dialects do not limit language development, either in the preschool years or in later school years. First, most children, even if they use a particular dialect, are hearing a variety of dialects used by peers and individuals in the media (television, movies, and so on). In addition, children typically are seeing only one version of English in print. Thus, all children are growing up in multiple-dialectal communities. What we think we hear (that is, everyone using SAE) just is not the case. We all are multi-dialectal in reality.

We are not suggesting that parents should not expose their children to what we know as standard English or discourage them from learning it. All children will need to understand and use the standard English used for academic purposes in the school setting. Thus, for children who speak a nonstandard dialect of English, it will be important for them to add a version of SAE to their repertoire without abandoning their nonstandard dialect. They also will need to learn when to use one dialect versus another. A recent situation we encountered is a good example of this point.

A student recently asked us how we would respond to the pronunciation of the word *picture* as *pitcher*. Apparently, a speech and debate teacher had deducted points because the student had used that pronunciation during a class presentation. We responded that we thought it would have been best to initially talk to the student about formal and informal pronunciations and the situations in which to use each. Then, we would have helped the student to see that a class presentation represents a setting that generally calls for standard English pronunciations. After developing the student's understanding of situational influences on pronunciation choices, we would hold him accountable for the production indicated by the setting. In other words, we would have discussed and coached first, and then in subsequent presentations, we would have expected him to use the SAE pronunciation, *picture*.

A parent's worry about the effects of a child's dialect on language, social, and academic development generally occurs because of a lack of knowledge about dialects. We hope this discussion of dialects has filled in some missing information. As we hope you have learned, we believe that parents can be excellent models for their children when it comes to understanding and respecting others' dialects. The value and importance a parent places on the communication abilities of any individual, regardless of his language abilities and dialect, will set an example for the child to follow.

> We believe that parents can be excellent models for their children when it comes to understanding and respecting others' dialects.

Culture and Language Development

AS YOU HAVE seen, the language of the family can play a large part in children's language learning. Parents who speak more than one language can provide additional experiences for their children during the language-learning years. Children learn more than just the speech sounds, words, and sentence structures of the family. They also learn the family's culture. In many cases, culture has an equally strong influence on language development, yet in ways that may not be as obvious as the way the family *speaks*. Differences in culture also may influence the manner in which children learn to talk.

In the popular media, such as television and movies, it is fairly common to see parents interacting with their children, talking to them and with them, focusing on what seems to be most important at the time. Indeed, in chapters 1 to 4, we have encouraged you to pay attention to your child's interests and converse about those topics. However, it is equally important to be aware of the type of upbringing you experienced, based on your particular cultural background, and how that upbringing may influence your interactions with your child. In addition, it is helpful to know your spouse's or your child's caregiver's cultural background, so as to best understand how these adults interact with young, developing children.

You or those around you may have come from a family or culture that did not encourage active communication with young children. Some cultures prefer that children remain silent and not talk with parents or other adults frequently. Although this may sound like the old adage, "Children should be seen and not heard," it is not that a cultural preference for quiet children means that children are not to be learning. Rather, a culture such as this places importance on reflection on what adults say and puts more emphasis on understanding language than using it. Children raised in those environments are equally good communicators as those from other cultures.

Some cultures may value storytelling; however, the structure of these stories may differ in form and purpose than those children encounter in popular books. For example, stories in popular books generally introduce main characters and move to some type of cause-and-effect plot. Many times, the purpose of the story is to entertain. However, people from other cultures tell tales or stories that are more historical in nature and serve to pass down their history.

Other cultural variations include how much parents require children to imitate them and how much they model conversational skills for their children. Some cultures encourage children to imitate everything that a parent says, rather than, as we suggested earlier, providing good language models and allowing the child to *choose* whether she will repeat some part of what the adult has said. Other cultures leave the learning of social language skills to friends or siblings, rather than through parent models. Still other cultures discourage eye contact with a conversational partner who is considered to be a superior. The differences in how cultures provide language-learning experiences to children can be many.

You may recognize some of these traits in your upbringing or that of your spouse or others who are raising young children such as yours. What are the implications of cultural variations on language development? In reality, not much! Children are naturally adept at learning language, regardless of the style of parent interaction or expectations. However, knowing and recognizing differences between parent-child interactions is important for two reasons.

First, if you find yourself following one of these traits, appreciate it for the value it represents in that culture. You are handing down to your child a significant part of you—your culture. Second, recognize that as your child nears his fifth year of life, if not sooner, he will be entering a more formal educational setting, such as preschool, kindergarten, and eventually, first grade. Knowing this, you can prepare him for these more "mainstream" situations by modeling and encouraging the use of language that is consistent with the "rules" of the school culture. Again, as we said earlier, this does not mean you should abandon your culture. Instead, you can *add* to your child's experiences and background by exposing him to the type of language use that may be expected in these more formal situations. Reviewing some of the suggestions we mentioned in chapters 1 to 4 should help with this endeavor.

Chapter Summary

GROWING UP IN bilingual or bidialectal homes does not put a child at greater risk for language-learning difficulties. These children will not be slower to develop language nor will it be a "harder" task. Quite the contrary, children who learn more than one language are perhaps better prepared to meet the demands of a multicultural, multilingual society. By understanding and promoting the importance of each language and dialect, parents have the capability of helping their children develop into respectful, knowledgeable citizens who honor differences and variations in others' language and styles of communication.

7

The Influence of Media on Language Development

DID YOU KNOW?

- The typical American child watches almost 25 hours of television a week.
- Computers may help or hinder language development.
- Video games may be one tool for children to practice their social language skills.

*H*elen and Tom allowed their children to play video games for one hour a day and watch television for one-and-a-half hours a day. Although they encouraged their children to do other things, such as read and play outside, it seemed that the children preferred the television or video game player to anything else. The more the parents watched their children engaged in these activities, the more they worried. When the children were watching television or playing video games, they almost seemed like zombies. The children *never talked or seemed to acknowledge others around them. When Helen suggested that perhaps television and video games should be discontinued, the children protested loudly. Even Tom wondered if that were best. How would the children fit in with other children if they weren't aware of the latest television shows or video games? Both parents were confused and felt helpless.*

Television . . . computers . . . videos. . . . Your child has so many types of "media" available at the push of a remote, the click of a mouse, or the swivel of a joystick. Did you know that the average amount of time children, even babies as young as two years old, spend in front of a television, computer, or video screen is over four hours per day? The average American child has two televisions, two VCRs, one video game player, and one computer in his home. But are these types of media "good" for him? Do they affect language development in a positive way? These not only are questions parents have asked us professionally but they also are questions we have asked ourselves in regard to our own children.

> Your child will be somewhat out of the loop if he cannot contribute to conversations on these media or demonstrate some competence with them.

One the one hand, it seems almost negligent not to allow your child to experience these different types of media. Most of his peers use these media, and your child will be somewhat out of the loop if he cannot contribute to conversations on these media or demonstrate some competence with them. On the other hand, these media have the potential to dominate your child's life to the extent that significant and important social interactions among his peers and adults may not occur.

As with the information on language development, we feel that your best tool to making decisions about what media your child should use and how much he should use them is a solid knowledge base about the effects of media on language development. With this knowledge in hand, you can begin to make intelligent and informed decisions about how your child uses different media. You also can become an expert in developing rich learning experiences that use these various media. Television, computers, and video games are powerful entities in your child's life. It's important that you control them so that they don't control your child.

Research on Media and Language Development

ONE THING YOU should keep in mind as we talk about the effects of media on language development is that there are many studies published and their results sometimes provide different views of the media. Some research suggests that the media can be helpful to your child's language and social development. Other studies bemoan the harmful effects of media on language development. In our opinion, the main factor that determines whether any type of media will be harmful to your child's growth is *you*. Just as your child is learning about the world around her through your language models and the daily situations to which you expose her, so, too, will she learn about language and the world of the media by what you allow her to view and how you interact with her as she uses the media.

There are two other points to keep in mind as we discuss the effects of media on your child's language development. First, much of the research on the effects of media on language development includes children considerably above the age of five years. This is most likely due to the rigors of participating in a research project. The information we discuss, though, is based mostly on what we know about the effects of media on the language development of infants, babies, toddlers, and preschoolers.

As for the other studies that address the effects of media on older children, we will leave those for another book!

Second, the research that addresses the effects of media on children's language development is quite diverse in the types of children studied. The information we present below involves children from low-income families to children from high-income families. These studies have also looked at children from a variety of cultural, racial, and language backgrounds, including children across all five continents! Globally, it seems everyone is interested in and perhaps concerned about the effects of media on language development. Thus, we can feel somewhat confident that the ideas we express on the influence of the media on your child's acquisition of language applies to you, your neighbor's child, and all children who watch, interact, or play with televisions, computers, and video games.

This chapter will provide some specific information about the effects of television, computers, and video games on your child's language development. And we conclude with some suggestions for how you can best take advantage of these media to help your child grow and learn while simultaneously ensuring that these media don't negatively affect your child's growth as a good communicator.

Television and Language Development

IN 1949, TEN years after being introduced to the general public, televisions were present in only 2 percent of American households. Today, 98 percent of American households own one. The average American child watches approximately 25 hours of television a week. Children who have a television in their bedroom, which includes about 20 percent of children who are preschoolers or younger, watch even more. In fact, other than sleeping, the average child spends more time watching television than at any other activity throughout the day. That's a lot of television! No wonder we as parents question its influence on our children. Although these average viewing times are probably excessive, you will see that television has some positive features that may aid your child's language development. However, like most other things, it also may lead to negative outcomes.

How Might Television Help Language Development?

Children are active viewers of television. Their little minds are often engaged in the actions and characters in the shows they watch. They like to discuss what they see and can recognize some of the objects and events on television as representations of those same objects and events in their own lives. In essence, the television can be, in some cases, the equivalent of a moving picture book. Thus, just as books can facilitate your child's language development, television has equal potential. However, just as your child needs your help in learning from books, he also needs your help to learn from television.

Television May Provide Speech and Language Models

Child language specialists have studied the type of language used in popular young children's shows, such as *Sesame Street, Mister Rogers' Neighborhood,* and *Teletubbies.* The findings are fascinating. Researchers have found that some of the language used includes the facilitative type of speech and language models known as child-directed speech (CDS) that we discussed in chapter 2. Just as parents use CDS with their young children, so, too, do some of the children's shows on television. Studies have shown that the CDS on some television shows promotes vocabulary development and preliteracy skills, such as letter identification.

Perhaps one of the best examples of CDS on a children's program is that of Mister Rogers. Listen to him some time. He either uses words that are familiar to his child audience or provides many examples of the meanings of words when he thinks the vocabulary may be new. He uses a slow, easy rate of speech when he talks. There is quite a bit of redundancy in the information he presents. As best he can, given the medium of television, he talks about actions and objects in the "here and now." Even his sentence structure is very simple; generally, he uses sentences with one verb, much like the sentence structure of toddlers. Obviously, Mister Rogers is not talking down to his audience. Rather, he is providing new information, much like you would with your child, in a manner that is interesting and helpful to young children.

Mister Rogers doesn't have the corner on being a good language model for children watching television. Other programs, such as *Sesame Street* and *Teletubbies*, also have similar episodes of CDS within their shows. Perhaps what's important to keep in mind here are the shows that tend *not* to use CDS in their dialogues or scripts. Often, these are cartoons and programs meant for adults (soap operas, sitcoms). These programs tend to have more adultlike conversations. True, when children watch these types of programs, they may get a laugh out of watching one character chase down another or a certain villainous character fall prey to frequent "accidents." However, these shows provide little help in developing a child's language skills because the language used is not developmentally appropriate for the young child. Not surprisingly, then, your job becomes one of determining how developmentally appropriate your child's television programs are.

So far, we have been discussing television in this section; however, the same principles apply to the viewing of movies, whether in a theater or on a home VCR. With the advent of VCRs, children have greater access to movies and likely gain more repeated exposures to movies than ever before. We've used family movies in our own homes as a way to facilitate the establishment of positive childhood memories and appreciation for routines. For example, when Caleb was about three years old, his mom and dad took him to Disneyland most Sunday afternoons. They took along the camcorder and filmed Caleb as well as some of the shows and performances. Interestingly, Caleb (at that age anyway) wasn't interested in television shows. He was quite interested, however, in viewing the videos of himself at Disneyland or the shows that he had seen at Disneyland. We would watch those over and over again and comment about his experiences. It was a great way to facilitate his use of language to refer to the "there and then," an important component of language development.

> Studies have shown that the child-directed speech on some television shows promotes vocabulary development and pre-literacy skills, such as letter identification.

Television May Enrich Playtime

Television also may be helpful for children's development of positive imaginative play. Children often will act out characters they have grown to know from television with their friends. In fact, your child may actually use what he sees on television as a basis for playing with his friends. Studies show that children may use the topics of television in a number of ways in their play. First, they may enhance their playacting with their friends, increasing the variety and fun of their regular play adventures. Second, children may use television themes to explore what they can do and how they can play. Children may take on the role of a television character by pretending to be that character, thus possibly extending the limits of what they have done in the past and perhaps challenging themselves to try new actions or methods of play.

So far in this book, we've offered several illustrations from the lives of our children. For this point, let us offer one from our own backgrounds. One of us (we'll let the reader cleverly decipher which one . . .) spent many hours pretending to be Samantha from the 1960s television show, *Bewitched*. She had some fun alone, imagining all sorts of delights that appeared with a simple twitch of her nose. Things were a lot more fun when her best friend, Leah, came to play. However, the presence of Leah did add a complication. Quite honestly, they both wanted to be Samantha. Fortunately, another television network developed a similar show, *I Dream of Jeannie*, about the same time. They negotiated, and Leah was happy to become Jeannie, probably because it was a lot easier to cross your arms and blink than it was to twitch your nose. In any case, the theme of "witch and genie" was carried through hours and hours of playtime between two childhood friends. In their world, Samantha and Jeannie were "moms who had to take care of babies," "wives who had husbands with jobs," and other scenarios that they observed in their own mothers' lives and on the television shows. All in all, these experiences with television led to rather rich "stories" that were enacted through pretend play.

Finally, a third way that television may increase play abilities is by increasing your child's socialization skills when playing with other children. When children select a theme for play based on a mutually viewed television show, they are able to develop and expand on a common ground or knowledge base.

It is not unlike when you are chatting with a colleague or coworker at your job site and you discover you have mutual interests. Not only does this allow you to increase the length and breadth of your conversations, it also may lead to other means of connecting (arranging a golf date, attending an arts and crafts show together). The same can be said for children who jointly engage in play focused on a television program they have watched. The familiarity of this theme allows them to expand and elaborate in their play, possibly resulting in more detailed, complex play situations.

> Television may increase play abilities by increasing your child's socialization skills when playing with other children.

Taken as a whole, then, television can be a positive influence in your child's development, especially as a means for social interaction with his peers during play. Play is an important skill, which is intricately connected to language development. Play is often a means for children to further develop high-level language skills, such as using and understanding more complex sentences or using groups of sentences related to one topic. Through cooperative and imaginative play, children learn to use language to negotiate with and manipulate others toward a common goal, as illustrated in our example of the two childhood friends negotiating to take on different television characters. In group play situations, children also learn to use language out of the here and now. Thus, play is a special situation that often allows children to learn and practice new language skills.

Television May Provide Exposure to Different Cultures and Languages

Interestingly, television also may influence your child's attitude and behaviors toward other children from different cultural and linguistic backgrounds. For example, researchers have studied with whom preschoolers choose to play after watching shows involving children from a variety of racial/cultural backgrounds. As it turns out, at least immediately after watching these "multicultural" shows, children are more apt to choose to play with children from any culture, either theirs or another. Those children who do not view multicultural programs are less likely to choose to play with children from outside their culture.

Although studies such as this do not have any direct impact on language development, one can argue that encouragement to play with children from different cultures leads not only to better understanding of others, but also to additional exposure to other languages and dialects. Such exposure can definitely contribute positively to language development. When children hear different words or different pronunciations for the same object or event, they begin to understand how languages differ and yet are used for the same purpose: communication. With this realization, they are beginning to think about language, that metalinguistic skill we mentioned in chapter 4 that is so important for developing reading and writing skills. Thus, children benefit both socially and in language development by hearing languages and dialects other than their own.

> Television has been shown to positively affect the language skills of children learning a second language.

Finally, television has been shown to positively affect the language skills of children learning a second language. Children who watch a television program based on another language can actually learn some of that second language via this medium. Of course, no child will learn a new language completely just by watching television. However, the audio and visual support of television can help preschoolers learn some rudimentary aspects of a second language.

How Might Television and Movies Hinder Language Development?

The helpful effects of television on your child's language development may be lessened considerably depending on a number of factors, including the length of time television is watched, how much she understands about the "reality" of the programs she watches, and the type of program and its content.

Not surprisingly, researchers have discovered that the more hours children watch television, the more likely they will demonstrate lower language abilities. This is true at least for the features of language that have been studied, such as sentence length and complexity and preliteracy skills. Why is this? Most language specialists would say that excessive television viewing takes away from social interactions between children and their parents and peers. It also may be that children are watching television programs that are not matched to their level of language understanding.

It is difficult to determine how much television watching is enough, but not too much, to benefit in the area of language development. One study found that children who watched as little as 15 minutes of a developmentally appropriate program per day had noticeably better language skills than children who watched "less sophisticated" programs, such as cartoons, for longer periods of time. Thus, large amounts of television watching, together with the viewing of developmentally inappropriate shows, may result in a less than optimal language-learning situation.

Young children may not always have a clear understanding for differentiating the television shows they watch from real life. When they are toddlers, children may not realize that what they see on television does not exist in the world. For example, they may assume Sesame Street is a real neighborhood. They also are less likely to understand that characters on television cannot hear or talk to them. What this research suggests is that young children are susceptible to believing that what is on television is real.

Why the concern about reality versus fantasy? It all may center on the content of a television program. When children watch shows with a great deal of conflict or aggression, they are more likely to imitate that conflict in social interactions. This may occur because, as toddlers, children do not always understand the "bigger" picture, or plot, of the story. Instead, they focus more on isolated incidents within stories. When toddlers view stories containing examples of violence or conflict, it is likely these individual events are remembered and acted out, rather than the larger story.

Research has shown that this attention to conflict and violence also extends to real-life depictions, such as nightly news programs. Preschoolers who watch nightly news programs may be at risk for experiencing more nightmares than children who do not watch these shows. For these children, the events that appear to be most frightening are those that involve violence by strangers or contain a great deal of visual coverage of destruction, such as natural disasters. Thus, it is important that you are aware of what your child is watching and the possible effects of that show on her. Some of the conflicts in everyday life can't be avoided. But as a knowledgeable parent, you can be aware of their effect on your child.

How do conflict and violence in the programs your child watches affect her language acquisition? In many ways, there may be no significant effect. Chances are, your child will have no problem acquiring different words or linking her thoughts together within more complex sentences. However, it may be that children who view acts of conflict and then act them out restrict the amount of social interaction they have with others (who wants to play with an aggressive peer?). Given this, the benefits of that interaction for social language development are lessened or lost completely. Because we know that children learn language best in situations that involve reciprocal interac-

tions, we want to ensure that children have every opportunity
to participate in these situations.

Summary of Television and Language Development

As parents and child language professionals, we suggest you be
neither complacent nor overreactive to the facts about television's effects on your child's language development. In reality,
the effect of television viewing on language development is a
double-edged sword. Too much viewing, and the "wrong" kind
of viewing, may impact your child's
language and social development in a
number of different and negative
ways. However, your child can actually learn new language skills, and
supplement those language skills already acquired, by watching developmentally appropriate television
shows. Your best approach to dealing
with this predicament is to be an active, knowledgeable guide of your
child's television viewing habits. At
the end of this chapter, we provide some additional suggestions
for how to handle this dilemma of television use.

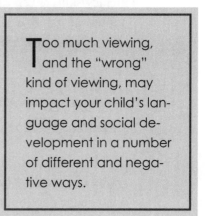

Too much viewing,
and the "wrong"
kind of viewing, may
impact your child's lan-
guage and social de-
velopment in a number
of different and nega-
tive ways.

Computers and Language Development

AS OF 1999, 69 percent of American households had a home
computer, and 43 percent of American homes had access to
the Internet. In fact, the average American child accesses the
Internet from home approximately four hours per week. This
last statistic most likely applies to older, school-age children
even though we both are personally aware of preschoolers who

have become quite sophisticated in accessing specific Web pages on the Internet. The point here is that access to computers, and also to the Internet, is something that the majority of young children in the United States have. In fact, children in preschool settings choose computer time during "free choice" almost 85 percent of the time.

As a parent of a child growing up in the third millennium, you undoubtedly have begun to wonder about the impact of computers on your child's language development. Indeed, it is not unusual to see a commercial or advertisement for a new computer program that will increase your child's language and literacy skills. Even though computers have been in American homes far less than televisions and movies have, we still have some idea of how their use may affect language development.

How Might Computers Help Language Development?

Children can best benefit from computer use when the programs involved are developmentally appropriate to their level of language development. In this case, developmentally appropriate not only means at a level of language that the child understands, it also means that the program is designed in a way that allows the child to explore the content of the program. Not all computer programs are designed this way.

Some computer programs follow a drill-and-practice format, requiring the child to practice one specific skill repeatedly to "get it right." The praise that the child receives suggests there is only one correct answer. Throughout these programs, the computer is in control of the learning. In essence, the child is a passive learner, simply responding to the computer versus actively engaging in the learning process. Common examples include programs that work on "memory" by presenting a sequence of two or three sounds, objects, or tones and having the child select buttons on a screen corresponding to those stimuli. The format goes like this: 1) computer presents stimulus; 2) child responds; 3) computer says "right" or "wrong." Granted few computer programs actually say, "WRONG." They use phrases like, "Try again" or "Nice try, but not right yet." However, the message is the same—the child has failed to do what the computer is requiring.

Other computer programs, however, require much more active participation from your child. These developmentally appropriate programs stimulate your child's physical, emotional, social, and cognitive growth through flexibility and variety in the ways they allow your child to respond. Children using these programs can explore and make choices within situations that represent familiar, everyday events in their lives. A "talking book" is a great example of this type of program. There are many programs on the market in which familiar children's stories are presented with animation that can be interactively explored. That is, each screen presents the story text along with animation elements that can be further selected, based on the child's interest.

It is these types of developmentally appropriate computer programs, then, that can help in language development because they mirror the types of good, language-learning situations your child encounters in other aspects of her life. Just as when she is exploring a new toy, learning a new game, or interacting with others to solve a problem, she can experience similar outcomes with appropriate types of computer programs, such as learning new vocabulary, relating thoughts across sentences, and talking about future situations. Studies have shown that developmentally appropriate programs can lead to higher scores on tests of language development.

Most computer programs involve multimedia presentations, or on-screen activity that involves sights, sounds, and words. One particularly positive outcome of these multimedia presentations is that children's preliteracy and literacy skills may be enhanced. With multimedia computer programs, preschoolers have the opportunity to link the visual aspect of words with the spoken form simultaneously. The "talking books" that we mentioned earlier usually highlight the words as they are read to the child. Older children, who are developing early reading skills, can take advantage of the opportunity to click on individual printed words or even phrases and hear them read aloud again. This allows the child to begin to associate a word that she knows with the printed version.

> One particularly positive outcome of these multimedia presentations is that children's preliteracy and literacy skills may be enhanced.

Given these capabilities, it may be tempting for parents to assume that a computer can take the place of the parent in book-reading activities. However, this would be a mistake. While the computer may be able to provide some experiences that help develop preliteracy skills, it will be unable to provide those experiences to the same breadth and depth that *you* can for your child. Thus, the usefulness of the computer for language learning should be viewed as a supplement, not a replacement, for your role in helping your child learn language.

The use of a computer necessarily involves several basic skills, such as the use of certain cognitive skills, visual-perceptual skills, and motor control skills. For example, children must be able to comprehend the use of symbols, so that when they see icons or images on the computer screen (for example, an hourglass or clock to indicate that the machine is processing information), they understand their meaning. Children also must be able to recognize that the symbols or pictures on the screen stand for objects in the real world. Finally, computer use generally involves fairly sophisticated use of a mouse, requiring the child to understand how to "point and click." Fortunately, research suggests that children as young as three years of age demonstrate all of these cognitive, visual, and motor skills.

These skills needed to use a computer are similar to the skills needed to access other "tools" of learning, such as books. When you think about it, a child must understand the symbols, or pictures, in a book, recognize them as standing for real objects, and be able to manipulate the pages of books to best benefit from book-reading experiences. Thus, computer use is one more way to practice and develop these skills. The skills themselves, whether used for computers or for books, are not language skills. Rather, they allow the child to better experience the language that is inherently part of that experience.

How Might Computers Hinder Language Development?

One danger with the use of computer programs is that children will devote more time to the computer and less time to noncomputer situations, especially those involving peers. Overuse of computer activities prohibits children from experiencing and using the social language skills they will need to become good conversationalists and communicators as they mature. Researchers have found that in homes where families rely almost solely on the computer for information and interaction and do very little book reading, the children tend to perform poorer than their peers on

One danger with the use of computer programs is that children will devote more time to the computer and less time to noncomputer situations, especially those involving peers.

measures of language skills. This fact alone shows the importance of *you* in *your* child's life.

Drill-and-practice computer programs, as mentioned earlier, also are not conducive to helping language develop. However, even multimedia presentations, those programs that tend to be supportive of learning because of the multiple sources of information, also may cause problems in language learning if designed inappropriately. Some multimedia computer programs pride themselves on the amount of extra auditory and visual effects present in the program. Take, for example, a computer program that is designed to increase a child's ability to tell stories. It may be developmentally appropriate in the language and cues given for the child, and it may follow the expected sequence of a story plot: problem, action, solution. However, the multimedia presentation may include extra animations, sound effects, or songs that are meant to maintain a child's attention. Unfortunately, in some cases, these bells and whistles distract from or interfere with the main purpose of the language experience. In this case, then, the child may benefit less from the experience of learning about the story format because he is more focused on creating sound effects or watching an animation that does little to further the plot of the story.

Summary of Computers and Language Development

More and more, computers are exciting tools and toys that most parents and children are likely to encounter on an almost daily basis. Having prepared this book on computers, we know firsthand what a lifesaver they are! As parents, we also know they have been valuable learning tools and creative toys for our children. As with television, you will need to understand how the computer can enhance your child's language development but also take away from experiences that might be more beneficial for your child. With your growing knowledge base in language development and the influence of computers on that development, you have the power to make wise decisions about your child's use of this type of media. We will provide you with some specific suggestions for computer use later. But first, let's review the effects of video game use on language development.

Video Games and Language Development

IT MAY SEEM odd that we would include this type of media in our discussion on factors that may influence language development. However, statistics show that 62 percent of all American homes have a video game player and that the average child spends up to seven hours a week playing video games. As parents, we sometimes feel we have *lived* these statistics! It is not unusual to hear the familiar *rings, dings, boofs,* and *gotchas* when you step into one of our homes. Our children are older than your child at this stage, but, like you, we wondered how these games might influence our children's development. Let's review, then, how video games might have a positive and not-so-positive impact on children's language development.

How Might Video Games Help Language Development?

Believe it or not, there are some positive aspects to those noisy games you hear in your den or in the car. Video games often are the first way your child becomes familiar with modern technology. Thus, the fine motor abilities and visual-spatial skills needed to participate in the task may pave the way for use of other types of technology, such as computers. More importantly for language development, many video games require a certain level of problem solving and logic as well as the ability to follow directions. Thus, although video games most likely won't be the way to facilitate language development, they may be tools for your child to use to practice understanding fairly complex sets of directions.

With some video games, there is a built-in need for interaction between two players. We see this as a positive aspect of video games and one that can help in language development. Given the right game, you can set up a situation where you and your child can jointly participate and focus on a common goal or topic. During this time, you can help your child's language to develop further by talking about the game, the directions, and how the game relates to his everyday activities, and by modeling appropriate levels of language. In other words, just like you do when the two of you are talking about *any* toy, video games have the potential for enabling a good, language-rich interaction to occur.

One of the special benefits of interaction regarding video games is that it places the child in the role of "teacher" or "facilitator" and the parent in the role of "learner." This can give your child several opportunities to consider another person's perspective and provide the appropriate amount and kind of information accordingly. Both Caleb and Caitlin tried faithfully to teach their mom the ins and outs of games, such as *Mario Brothers*. It was quite apparent in these situations that the children's visual and spatial memories, as well as their eye-hand coordination, far surpassed their moms'. It was a nice change for them to get to be the experienced ones, the ones in the conversation to be instructing, facilitating, and so on. Of course, they also got to see what it was like to have a student who wasn't always optimally attentive!

Opportunities for interaction set video games apart from other media, such as television. Television is a fairly noninteractive activity. Most people just sit and watch it. Typically, little interaction occurs between parent and child during television viewing (but see our suggestions below!). However, video games either require two players at a time or provide a great chance for the child to teach someone else how to play. These opportunities for active learning and interaction are definitely a plus!

How Might Video Games Hinder Language Development?

Just as there are video games that encourage critical thinking, problem solving, and interaction among participants, there also are games that encourage social isolation of the player from others. Children who play games that are for single players for excessive amounts of time are, by definition, decreasing the amount of time they can spend in social interactions with their peers. As we mentioned previously, this may adversely affect language development because these children are not receiving the language models and play interactions upon which further language acquisition is built.

Similarly, some games do not require any type of active involvement of the mind, other than to shoot a character on the screen or jump one more hurdle. With excessive amounts of this type of play, a child is decreasing the opportunities he has to engage in other activities that are more beneficial to language development. Language is a means for solving problems in our heads. That is, we often will talk to ourselves, either within our minds or aloud, to help figure out a solution to a problem. When little thinking is involved in a video game, then that means less opportunities to practice using language for critical thinking activities. Just like any other skill, additional practice leads to better development and performance.

Now, some parents might think that there is no real harm in their child occasionally playing one-person games or games with little creative thinking required. They are probably right. However, as children become more entrenched in the playing of video games, what used to be occasional occurrences may soon become more frequent occurrences. It is at that point that parents need to be concerned whether their children are participating in situations that encourage and facilitate further language use and development or becoming socially isolated.

Finally, just as some young children have a difficult time separating fantasy from reality on television, so, too, do they have difficulty separating animated violence in video games from real violence. Studies show that children who play excessive amounts of violent video games may demonstrate more aggression in their play with others. Certainly, this type of behavior is not conducive to developing social language skills within play situations.

Summary of Video Games and Language Development

Video games are no different in many respects from television or computers. They can contribute to your child's language development, and they can diminish the usefulness of the experience. As parents, if you consider these games mostly as another toy you can use to play *with* your child, then chances are your child will reap the benefits of this type of media. You are an informed parent, so making decisions about the types of video games your child uses should become quite easy. We also provide some concrete ideas to follow to help you make some decisions about video games, computers, and television use by your child. Isn't it amazing how many issues you have to consider as a parent? At least you know, though, that the major benefactor of all of this knowledge-building is your child.

Your Role in Your Child's Use of Media

THE RESEARCH SPEAKS loudly and clearly. All three of these types of media can be helpful to your child's language and social development if used correctly and wisely. As you think specifically about your child's use of media, there are a few key points to keep in mind for each type of media.

Your Child's Use of the Television

Your child has many television shows from which to choose. Some of these programs will be educationally and developmentally appropriate for your child and others will not. Television has a ratings system now, but we have found that the best way to determine what is right for your child is for you to either preview an episode of the show before your child watches future episodes or view the show with her. Only then will you be sure that your child's time in front of the television is useful.

> The best way to determine what is right for your child is for you to either preview an episode of the show before your child watches future episodes or view the show with her.

As you watch television with your child, keep in mind that you want to explain and discuss what your child is thinking about the programs she watches. Also, just as you do during your book-reading time, you can draw links between the "unreal" world of television and the real world of the child's everyday experiences. We find a good time for this discussion is during commercials or by pausing a video temporarily. An exchange might go something like this:

Dad: "Wow. This is exciting. Tell me what you think about the show so far."

Child: "That bear is a bad bear. He's mean."

Dad: "Yes, he is. Do you think that all bears are like that?"

Child: "I don't know."

Dad: "Well, sometimes, bears can be mean, but many times they aren't. I learned from books that the best thing to do is to watch them from far away . . . or in a zoo. Do you think we have bears around here?"

Child: "Yeah, just like that one on TV."

Dad: "Well, actually, that bear isn't from around here. This is a movie from a place far away. The only bears close by us are in the zoo. Remember when we went to the zoo? We saw those bears? They were safe in a special area, where we could see them, but not be too near them."

In this exchange, the father is helping the child to learn that the program is not representative of where she lives, broadening her understanding of the topic, indirectly showing the importance of book reading, and engaging the child in thinking about what she is watching. All of these are strategies that will enhance television viewing.

As a parent of a young child, you also can begin to set up viewing habits that will develop a realistic relationship with the television. For example, you want to discourage watching television during mealtimes. If you recall from chapter 4, mealtimes are actually great times to develop preliteracy skills, as well as for engaging your child in conversations. These activities are very difficult to do if one or both of you are focused on the television screen. Also, set certain limits for television viewing. The American Academy of Pediatrics suggests no more than one to two hours per day, which is less than half of what the average American child watches. With limited television time, your child will have additional time for the experiences that can strongly influence language development, such as dialogues with you or play interactions with her peers.

Finally, when setting up daily rituals, consider leaving the last few minutes of the day, the bedtime minutes, for quality book reading and talking with you. Studies show that parents who read to their children are more likely to have children who grow up to be readers themselves. In addition, this time, which typically is a calming down time, allows your child to focus on the language of the book and the models you use to link the book to her everyday experiences. What a wonderful and fruitful way to end the day!

Your Child's Use of the Computer

As with television, you want to be fully aware of what your child does on the family computer. Many times you have control of this because you buy the computer programs that will be used. With the increase in relatively low-cost computer programs, parents have many choices when buying programs for their child. Consider the content and purpose of the computer program you might purchase. Is it geared toward educating your child, or just entertaining? Both can be enjoyable, and both can be learning experiences, so it makes sense to have both kinds of programs available to your child. Is the purpose of the program to drill and practice a specific skill, or is it to allow your child to explore and solve problems as he interacts with the program? It will be these latter programs that enhance your child's language development and make his time spent on the computer well worth it.

Talk to your child about the purpose of the program. You will find it is fascinating what your child is learning, or not learning, as the case may be. Remember, sometimes programs distract the child from the real learning experience. Take, for example, the following scenario:

Mother: "That's a fun little story. Tell me what you learned from it."

Child: "If you click the dog's tail, it wags, but if you click on its mouth, it barks really loud!"

Mother: "Yes, that does happen. What about the story? What happens with the dog?"

Child: "He will keep barking each time you click on his mouth."

Mother: "Yes. But didn't he lose his bone? What happens when he loses his bone?"

Child: "I don't remember."

Mother: "Well, let's go through it together and see if we can figure it out ourselves."

This short scenario emphasizes how a well-meaning program can mislead a child about its purpose. In this case, the excitement of making the dog bark and wag its tail has overshadowed the experience of learning about the problem, the action, and the solution. Luckily, the mother is there to help the child appreciate what he can learn from the computer program.

Finally, you also want to consider setting some guidelines for computer use. If you have a computer with Internet access, monitor your child's use of it. There are many programs available to parents that allow them to block parts of the Internet that are unsuitable and inappropriate for their child. Place the computer in a location of the house where you can see what your child is doing. By doing this, you more likely will be aware of what your child is seeing and playing on the computer.

Your Child's Use of Video Games

We have gone into video game or movie rental stores with our children and seen the sheer volume of video games available. It is staggering! However, you have the tools to help you and your child make wise decisions about which games to choose.

First, consider video games that allow multiple players at the same time. As we said before, this likely will lead to more social interactions. Also, read the description of the game on the box. Does the game involve thinking and problem solving? If so, not only will your child's hands be working, but her mind will be, too. Games that require thinking

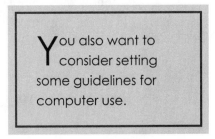

You also want to consider setting some guidelines for computer use.

skills also allow you to model for your child how you can use language to solve problems. This is easily done by "thinking aloud." For example:

Parent: "This is hard. It seems like I have to be smarter than the wizard. Okay, I'm thinking I should try and sneak the jewels into the castle. What do you think?"

Child: "If you do that, you need something to hide them."

Parent: "Okay, good point. I see several things around me. I could use a box, but it is too big. I could use my pockets in my jacket, but they are too small. Hmm, I'm still thinking, are you?"

Child: "Yeah! Why don't you use the bag?"

Parent: "Good idea. Now, let's talk about our next problem."

This little dialogue not only shows how language can be used to convey how you think, but it also emphasizes another important point: Play *with* your child using this media of video games. Just as you join in on other play activities, you can engage in this play as well.

Finally, just as with the other types of media, be aware of what options you and your child have. You can limit the amount of time spent with video games so that there is plenty of time to play nonvideo–game activities. You can keep the video game player, and other media, out of your child's bedroom. Remember, increased access can lead to playing to excess. You also can be knowledgeable about the content of the games.

You may be aware that video games now have ratings to help parents determine appropriateness for their child's use. Often, even the picture on the front cover will help you decide this! If you follow these simple suggestions, we bet your child will obtain all the benefits of video games for language development with few or none of the drawbacks.

Chapter Summary

THE MOST IMPORTANT point to keep in mind is that you have the tools to make these media helpful and important for your child. You know how to monitor the content of these media, and how important it is to talk about what your child views. You know to discuss whether the actions he sees on the screen are similar to real-life experiences or not, and how possibly aggressive or violent actions are potentially dangerous and inappropriate in everyday situations.

You also know that it is important to provide alternative, "nonmedia" activities to enhance your child's language development, because these experiences will far outweigh those from media experiences. Engaging in all activities as a family shows you are committed to making the most out of all situations you encounter.

Finally, don't forget what we talked about in chapters 1 to 4. Using media is no different from using other objects in this world when it comes to helping your child develop language. If you know how language develops, and you use that knowledge in practical, meaningful, everyday situations, your child will benefit greatly.

8

Language
Development
and Childcare

> **DID YOU KNOW?**
>
> - The educational background of a childcare provider can affect a child's language development.
>
> - Simple household items like kitchen utensils, pots, and pans may be more beneficial to children's language development than fancy toys.
>
> - The number of children per childcare provider may affect children's language development.

*D*addy, don't leave! I want to go with youuu. . . . Daddy, I love you. . . . No, Daddy . . . Don't goooooooooo."*

These words were spoken . . . well . . . screamed . . . by Genevieve every day for the first three weeks of her first experience with out-of-the-home childcare. They pretty much broke the heart of her father. She was only three. He was abandoning her. Her tears were flooding the childcare center. How could he be so insensitive?

In fact, this association between tears and screams and excruciating pangs of guilt continued until about halfway through the third week, when Genevieve's childcare provider informed her father that as soon as he was out of sight, she immediately stopped crying and started playing with her peers.

Although the guilt somewhat diminished, her father was still bothered by the overriding question. Should parents really place their child in childcare? What are the effects of childcare on a child? Most important for this book and for this particular father, what are the effects of childcare on the language development of young children? The purpose of this chapter is to provide the answer to this last question. We will review the factors that make childcare situations effective, and noneffective, in furthering your child's acquisition of language. In addition, we will provide you with some ideas for how you can determine whether a particular childcare situation best meets your child's needs, given her age.

Like the information we presented in chapter 7 on the media, the research in the area of childcare and language development spans many different types of families, families that vary in socioeconomic status, culture, and education. Studies have been conducted in childcare programs based in homes, as well as in public and private childcare facilities. Thus, the information we provide should be relevant to almost all situations in which you might find yourself when searching for childcare.

When it comes down to the bottom line, the most important factor in your child's childcare situation and its effects on language development is *quality adult language stimulation.* Thus, whether your child receives it from you as a stay-home parent, or from you as a working parent in collaboration with her childcare provider, your child's language development will be enhanced when the adults around her know about language development and use age-appropriate strategies. So, let's begin looking at this situation of childcare and what seems to be most crucial for your child's development.

Research on the Effects of Childcare on Language Development

CAN A CHILDCARE situation positively, or negatively, affect language development? The answer to this question is yes in both ways. Researchers have been studying the effects of childcare on children's development for quite some time, and the results are very interesting. But before we share those with you, let's take a few minutes to talk about *how* researchers look at childcare situations to determine what works and what doesn't work.

Most childcare situations (in-home care, public or private childcare, and preschool) are judged in a number of ways, including: (a) appropriateness of activities; (b) provider-child ratio (the number of children for which a provider is responsible);

> The most important factor in your child's childcare situation and its effects on language development is quality adult language stimulation.

(c) the quality of the provider-child and child-child interactions; and (d) the physical environment of the care facility. These situations have been judged in relationship to various characteristics of the children who are enrolled in the programs, such as their language skills and play behaviors. Sometimes, childcare environments are judged simply through observations. Other times, they are rated by performances on tests or by questionnaires. Some studies even try to compare childcare facilities that have different philosophies.

The point we make here is that our review of childcare and its effect on language development comes from a number of studies that have looked at the situation in a variety of ways. We will try to provide you with the main facts, regardless of how the researchers studied the childcare situation and what type of situation it was. We have organized this information around three main aspects of childcare that can positively impact language development: the providers, the environment, and the curriculum (the activities and philosophy of the provider).

What to Look for in Childcare Providers

SPEAKING AS PARENTS, we believe the main feature to look for in your child's care provider is warmth and a genuine interest in your child. Nothing can lead to stifled development more than a childcare provider who shows little care, affection, compassion, and positive regard for your child and his development. We know of no way to measure this other than to use your good, parental feelings and intuitions. However, besides providing affection and attention to your child, you also want to ensure that the provider will help your child's language develop.

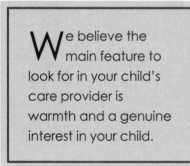

We believe the main feature to look for in your child's care provider is warmth and a genuine interest in your child.

Studies have shown, perhaps not surprisingly, that one of the best features in a childcare provider for helping your child acquire language is an understanding of child development. If your childcare provider is strongly grounded in her knowledge of how children develop, chances are your child will score better on tests of language development than children who have providers who have little understanding of typical development in children.

The educational level of providers is strongly tied to their understanding of child development. For the most part, children who have childcare providers who have higher levels of education (beyond high school) will score better on language tests than their peers. This is especially true for providers who have some type of teacher or educational certification, although this is not necessary to be an informed and knowledgeable provider.

What is it that more knowledgeable providers do that sets them apart from less educated providers? All the research suggests that educated providers are more likely to understand how to fine-tune their interactions and activities to the needs of the individual child, your child. Researchers call this taking advantage of "teachable moments," those times when it seems the child is ready and willing to learn something new. Instead of providing activities or toys that re-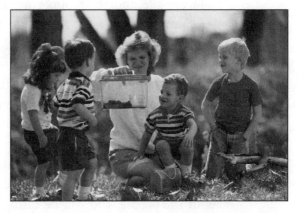quire all children to play in the same way regardless of their developmental level, educated providers are able to tailor an activity or use of a toy to best help your child develop the skills that are next to be learned. In essence, educated providers interact with children just as we discussed in chapters 1 to 4. They follow the child's lead in play and language, provide models of language at or just above the level of the child, and show respect and understanding for what the child says.

Of course, a provider's knowledge and education about language and child development should not be static. A provider cannot simply take one or two classes on child development and have all of the information that will ever be needed. Like other individuals involved in health and education, childcare providers should be periodically updating their knowledge base. Some public and private childcare facilities allow this, offering providers workshops or time off to attend conferences so they can increase their understanding of child development and current "best practices." Childcare providers also have opportunities to learn new information via the Internet. The number of Web sites dedicated to this topic is phenomenal. Thus, it will be important that you determine whether the prospective childcare site values continuing education.

To best help your child's language develop while he is in childcare, then, you will want to think about several factors surrounding the provider. You will want to inquire about the educational level and certification status of the providers at the childcare site and their opportunities for continuing education. You also will want to determine whether the providers have a background in child development, including, it is hoped, language development. Finally, you will need to determine how much attention and care the providers typically give the children at the site. Perhaps your best way to determine this last feature is to observe the providers at different parts of the day as well as question other parents whose children currently attend the childcare center. By investigating these aspects of the childcare site, you can begin to develop an opinion about the people who will be caring for your child while you are away.

What to Look for in Childcare Facilities

WHEN WE WERE considering different childcare options for our children, one of our first criteria was that it had to be clean, light, open, and welcoming. However, we also looked for other factors that have been shown to be effective for language development. First, we looked at the materials that were available to the children in the childcare site. We wanted a variety of toys and materials that could encourage the use of our child's imagination. Interestingly, one of the best ways to encourage imagination and increase a child's use and understanding of language is the presence of toys and play areas that mirror everyday situations. We also determined the number of children assigned to any one childcare provider. The ratio of students to teacher may influence the quality and quantity of language models your child receives.

Play Materials and Learning Events

For some time, researchers have known that children can learn and use more language when they are engaged in games and activities for which they have some prior knowledge. Most children, even by the age of two, have developed some fairly good ideas about familiar situations, such as grocery shopping, birthday parties, trips to McDonald's, and so forth. This knowledge about familiar events is called script knowledge (recall our discussion of scripted events in chapter 3). Scripts contain all the information children have about the people and objects involved in the situation, what actions happen, and possibly the order of the actions that occur. When a child has a good understanding of how events occur and who does what, this means the child can concentrate more on the language that is used to talk about or converse within those situations.

Think about your own experiences as an adult. Most likely, the first time you tried to line dance or play chess, you struggled so much with learning the objects and actions involved, that you had a hard time talking during the activity. However, the more you continued to participate in these activities, the more the objects and actions became familiar. Pretty soon, you were probably talking about "ball and chains" and "cross-overs," or you were able to talk about the day's events while taking your opponent's pawn! The same is true for children. The more they know about an event, the more they can converse during the activity and use the specialized language terms involved.

Now, this doesn't mean that children should not be asked to play with toys or participate in situations with which they have little experience. If we said this, children would never learn all the wonderful things they do about this world! Rather, this means that helpful childcare sites have plenty of toys and play areas that capitalize on children's knowledge of familiar events, their script knowledge, so that the children have multiple opportunities to learn about and use language without the burden of learning a new activity. Childcare sites that have scripted play areas are more likely to have children who maintain topics of conversation longer, ask for more clarifications for understanding, and demonstrate more social play behaviors than childcares without these play areas.

Of course, what might be a scripted play situation for one child may not be a scripted play situation for another. For example, a play area modeled after a school setting would be inappropriate for children who have not yet attended school. Children who are growing up in rural areas might benefit from areas, or "centers" (specific areas of play), that are devoted to farm life, with toys and houses that represent those found on a farm. Conversely, children in urban areas might benefit more from toys and activities that reflect their everyday lives, including large street maps, cars, buses, and trucks representing a downtown scene. Moreover, most children, by the age of four, should have some familiarity with events and situations dealing with acts of literacy (reading, writing, spelling). It is these types of play situations that also have been shown to be very beneficial to children's language development.

Childcare facilities that include centers where literacy actions (pretend reading or writing) can occur using the tools of literacy (paper, pencils, crayons, books, and so on) tend to have children who score higher on tests of language and literacy. This makes a lot of sense. These childcare centers, in essence, are creating "high-print" environments. We have seen childcare facilities that have centers based on the post office or grocery stores. Children play in these centers, "writing" notes, sticking them in envelopes, and mailing them. They "write" lists of needed items and then shop for the items, "reading" the items on the list and crossing them off after each item is put into the shopping cart. These types of play experiences reinforce children's understanding of the events while simultaneously providing them experience in literacy events, something we talked about as crucial in chapter 4. The more experiences children have with literacy, the better prepared they will be as they enter formal schooling. Keep in mind children do not need formal reading or writing instruction at this stage of development. In fact, most children do not have the prerequisite skills needed for this. That is why activities focused on preliteracy skills will best help your preschooler's language and literacy skills develop.

> Childcare facilities that include centers where literacy actions (pretend reading or writing) can occur using the tools of literacy (paper, pencils, crayons, books, and so on) tend to have children who score higher on tests of language and literacy.

Most childcare sites offer more than just literacy and play experiences. For example, there is a very good chance that the childcare facility you observe will provide television, or videos, for the children in its care. A national survey found that 86 percent of childcare facilities in the United States use live television or videotapes. If you've read chapter 7, you will know that television in and of itself is not a negative contributor to language development. Rather, it is what is watched, and how long it is watched, that can affect language development. Thus, it will be highly important for you to know whether the television is used as just one means for helping your child develop or as a time filler so that adults do not need to interact with the children.

Finally, you will want to determine whether the providers consider childcare to go beyond just their facility. Quality childcare providers recognize the importance and impact of the family on developing children, so they attempt to include parents and siblings as much as possible. Involving parents and other family members, either by encouraging volunteerism at the site or by providing means for the family to be better informed of what the child does while at the site, may increase the quality and quantity of rich, language-learning experiences. For example, one group of researchers examined the effect of parents' knowledge of their child's daily activities on language use. On alternating days, children left the childcare facility with materials that were either "child-focused" (art projects completed by the child, souvenirs from field trips) or just their personal items (coats, lunch bag). The researchers then audio-recorded the parent-child conversations held in the car on the way home. They found that when the parent and child had the child-focused materials to discuss, the language used by the child was more mature. The children maintained the conversational topic longer, and the parents were able to question and comment more. Thus, in very simple ways, childcare providers and parents can extend the benefits of childcare beyond the four walls of the facility.

As you tour a prospective childcare facility, ask yourself about these key elements. Does the facility include centers or play areas that contain toys and materials representative of the familiar events in your child's life? Will your child have at least some knowledge of the types of toys available? Does the facility provide opportunities for toddlers and preschoolers to play with materials that are used for the literacy acts of reading, writing, and spelling? Does the facility limit the amount of television watched and have appropriate guidelines for the type of programs provided? Are parents encouraged to be active in their child's childcare experiences? If you are answering yes to most or all of these questions, then chances are you have found a childcare site whose environment is conducive to your child's further language development.

> Does the facility limit the amount of television watched and have appropriate guidelines for the type of programs provided?

Provider-to-Child Ratios

Considerable research is available examining provider-to-child ratios. Ratios of 1-to-7 or less are considered desirable for toddlers and preschoolers. The ratio is considerably less for younger children. Infants should have a ratio of 1-to-1 or 1-to-2. Babies may have a ratio of 1-to-3 or 1-to-4. Results from several studies suggest that smaller provider-to-child ratios lead to better overall language development for the children involved. In addition to adult-to-child ratios, you should also consider the overall number of children in attendance. Even if a facility offers a provider-to-child ratio of one adult to six children, three adults with a group of eighteen children would be considered large and not beneficial to language development. The larger the group, the lower the scores on tests of language development. In fact, children who are cared for in large groups may use fewer words per sentence, fewer different words, and talk at a different rate than children in smaller groups.

What is it about larger provider-child ratios and large groups that hinder language development? The answer can be summarized easily; there is a lack of quality interaction between the adult and the children. When an adult is responsible for many children, there is little time to meet the needs of individual children. The adult is no longer able to easily follow a child's lead in a conversation, determine the focus of a child's attention and talk about it, or provide meaningful models of language that are just above the level that each particular child is capable of producing. The research shows that most adults who find themselves trying to interact with a large group of young children spend a great deal of time organizing and managing the group, rather than in quality interactions with the children.

What to Look for in the Childcare Curriculum

THE CURRICULUM OF a childcare facility primarily refers to the activities provided. Some childcare facilities emphasize a direct instruction curriculum, where children are presented information in a traditional "teacher-student" mode and maybe even tested on the material. Other sites provide a more open-atmosphere curriculum, in which children are expected to learn when they are ready to learn. In this type of curriculum, the provider supports the child in whatever she wants to do or learn, but provides little direction. Finally, other childcare facilities may follow a type of "hybrid" curriculum that views learning as an interaction between directed instruction from the adult and activities chosen by the child. In these situations, the adult sets up activities specific to certain types of learning, and then guides, as opposed to teaching, the child to learn new information and expand on known information.

Perhaps the differences among these three styles can best be exemplified using a book-reading activity. In a direct instruction situation, a provider would have a goal of teaching reading. She may use drill cards to teach certain words or letters, or she may read a book and then require the children to answer questions to check for understanding or comprehension. The focus would be similar to traditional school classrooms, where the provider teaches, asks a question, then judges the answer.

In an open-atmosphere curriculum, a provider would read books to the children, but not necessarily ask questions about the book or check for comprehension. If a child asked about something in the book, however, the provider would respond with the needed information. In this case, the child determines what will be gained from the book reading. It may even be that the child does not want to listen to the book reading, choosing to engage in some other activity instead.

Finally, in the hybrid curriculum, a provider would read a book, knowing the level of the children and what they might need to learn new language or literacy skills. For example, if she thought the children were ready to start using their knowledge of story plots to predict what happens in stories, she might first model, and then ask the students to predict upcoming events in a story. If she felt the students were ready to learn more about letter sounds, she might make comments about how certain words start with the same sounds, either as she read the book or after she had completed reading the book and was reviewing it. In all cases, she would guide the students, through her models of language and thought-provoking, leading statements, to higher levels of understanding of language and literacy.

The research shows that for young children, up through the preschool years, the direct instruction curriculum is least effective in helping them learn. The other two types of curriculum can both be helpful, most likely at different times or in different situations. For example, it may be that the open-atmosphere curriculum is most helpful when children are first exploring new situations and new toys, where their focus will naturally be on learning how the particular activity or object works. This approach appears to allow more child-to-child interactions, which have been shown to encourage longer sentences. Conversely, the hybrid curriculum is likely best for when children are engaged in activities that are somewhat familiar and ready to learn more about those situations. In these situations, there will be more adult-to-child interactions, which have been shown to increase children's conversational turn-taking and use of complex language skills, reduce the number of gaps between conversational turns, and lead to greater use of language to solve problems.

As you can probably guess, these last two types of curriculum best meet what we feel are appropriate types of language-learning situations. They reflect what we said in chapters 1 to 4. Just as we suggested that you follow your child's lead in conversations, model appropriate types of language, and so on, so, too, should the providers for your child.

The curriculum of a childcare facility is crucial. No matter how educated a provider is, if she must provide for too many children at one time and has little flexibility in meeting the needs of the children, she will not be helpful in further developing your child's language. Thus, as you observe different childcare facilities, observe the size groups they provide and the number of adults per children in those groups. Ask about the facility's philosophy of care and education, and determine how well you think it matches what is known to be beneficial to acquiring language. By becoming an informed and knowledgeable parent about the providers, the childcare site, and the curriculum, you will be ready to make appropriate and important decisions about your child's care.

What Childcare Is Best for My Child?

AS YOU MIGHT guess, if we could provide the definitive truth in answer to this question, we would be touring the world doing seminars devoted solely to this topic! Instead, the best answer will need to come from you. As you contemplate this answer, we encourage you to think about the information we have provided, and combine that information with what you learned in chapters 1 to 4. Undoubtedly, just as we discovered, you will find your answer will vary somewhat with your family's specific needs, as well as the age of your child. In the last few pages of this chapter, we provide some suggestions regarding what to look for in a childcare situation and what to ask depending on the age of your child. We start off each developmental stage with a scenario of a childcare facility. Read that scenario and then determine whether you think it is appropriate before reading our answer. Let's see how much you have learned!

> No matter how educated a provider is, if she must provide for too many children at one time and has little flexibility in meeting the needs of the children, she will not be helpful in further developing your child's language.

What Type of Childcare Is Best for My Infant?

Mr. and Mrs. Dailey are looking for a childcare facility for their six-month-old daughter, Heather. As they enter one site, they notice that it is bright and clean and has a wonderful, homelike atmosphere to it. There are several rooms to the childcare facility, one that is specific to infants. Observing the room, they see that there are several adults, up to three, in the room at any given time. Each of the twelve cribs appears clean and well kept. There are bright posters on the wall and cute, little mobiles hanging over each crib and over the changing tables as well. There are several rocking chairs and some blankets on the floor for the infants to lie on and play with toys. As the Daileys talk with some of the providers, they learn that each woman seems very warm and friendly and each has been providing care for over 10 years. The director of the childcare emphasizes that the infant providers are all women who have had their own children and are experienced in childcare.

What do you think? Is this an appropriate setting for little Heather? Are there any concerns or questions you have? The facility seems clean and the providers well intentioned. There appear to be visual stimuli for the children to look at and toys for the children to manipulate. However, looking at the information provided, we definitely have some questions and concerns.

First, we worry about the provider-to-infant ratio. If all the cribs were filled, the ratio, at best, would be one provider to every four infants. This would be quite high. In addition, the size of the group, twelve infants, suggests that individualized attention would be scarce. Remember, infants are fascinated with the human face and voice and can learn a great deal about language by interacting with an adult. With such a large group and large provider-infant ratio, we wonder how likely it will be that the providers can encourage joint attention with the infants, engage them in playful babbling back and forth, and follow their interests and visual gaze and make it the topic of a conversation.

We also wonder, and would require more information, about the providers' level of education and understanding of development. As you know from reading chapter 1, the first year of life involves an incredible amount of learning. Experience can provide a lot of knowledge regarding child development. However, we wonder how much the providers are aware of the special skills that infants have and develop during the first year of life, such as their preference for differences in shapes, contours, and shadowing; their developing ability to babble in more mature ways; and their use of gestures and vocalizations to comment and question, to name a few.

The point here is not to put down this particular childcare facility. Chances are, the providers are well meaning and full of care for the infants in their charge. However, as a parent, you want to consider all the facts before deciding where your child will spend a large portion of her day. So, as you look for childcare for your infant, make sure that there is an adequate provider-infant ratio, a small group, and an educated and caring set of providers.

What Type of Childcare Is Best for My Baby?

Mrs. Dodds has a neighbor, Virginia, who provides childcare in her home. She has known Virginia for some time and considers her bright (she went to community college for two years) and thoughtful. When she started offering childcare, Virginia mentioned that she had joined an Internet group for in-home childcare providers so that she could stay up on current practices in childcare. Virginia takes care of her own 19-month-old son and a 23-month-old niece. She has turned her den into her childcare room. There are plenty of windows to allow in light and plenty of toys, including large-size dolls, cars, a house and furniture, a play kitchen with kitchen materials, and a large shelf of children's books. She lets the children watch Sesame Street *once every morning and afternoon. Virginia prides herself on cleanliness and ensures that she constantly washes her hands after helping each child with his or her food and toileting needs.*

Mrs. Dodds is trying to decide whether she should let Virginia care for her 22-month-old son. What do you think?

Though we might ask a few more questions, like you, we are feeling very confident about this situation and its helpful influence on language development. In this case, the provider, Virginia, appears to be eager to educate herself on what the children might need for learning. She has stocked her play areas with toys that should be familiar to the children, allowing scripted play to occur. The ratio of provider to baby is relatively small and the entire group is small. The environment seems conducive to learning.

Given this, we still would like to observe Virginia and determine how she interacts with the children. Does she spend all her time with them, following their leads, letting them explore new toys and play together with familiar toys? Will she be adding any extra children? What is her policy for Mrs. Dodds popping in to play with the children and will she keep Mrs. Dodds aware of what her son does on a daily basis? Depending on the answers to these questions, this particular childcare situation seems like a good choice.

While you may not place your child in an in-home childcare setting, the same qualities evident in Virginia's home are important for any site. Your childcare provider needs to be aware of the new language skills your baby is acquiring. During this time, your baby will be using one-word sentences, so his care provider needs to know how important it is to repeat and expand on what he says, to help him bridge to the next level of language development, which is multiword sentences. The provider should be setting good speech models for your child, not expecting him to say all the speech sounds in the words he uses correctly, but saying the word back to your child with the correct pronunciation. With this knowledge of language development and the appropriate environment, your baby should benefit from the interactions he encounters in his childcare setting.

What Type of Childcare Is Best for My Toddler?

Claire is three-and-a-half years old. She has stayed home with her mother up until now, but her mother, Joanne, has decided to return to working outside the home, so Joanne and Claire's dad, Fred, are shopping around for an appropriate childcare placement. On this particular day, they visit the childcare associated with Fred's corporation. They have heard excellent feedback about it from other parents whose children attend this facility, which maintains a provider-child ratio of 1-to-6. The information they hear about the program seems to make it an ideal choice. It is known for its attention to detail, both in meeting the standards of health and safety and in meeting the individual needs of the children involved.

As they look around the room, they see areas devoted to centers: a grocery market center, a bill-writing center, a library with many different children's books, and an art center. There is also a large area devoted to free play, including blocks, houses and dolls, pretend household items, small balls, and so on. They notice on one bulletin board that there is a certain schedule to the day, involving free-play time, circle time for sharing, center time, lunch time, book-reading time, and nap time. As they

> The provider should be setting good speech models for your child, not expecting him to say all the speech sounds in the words he uses correctly, but saying the word back to your child with the correct pronunciation.

came into the room, they read the parents' board, which indicated, among other things, that some of the providers would be attending an upcoming workshop at the local community college on new findings in child development. The director of the program, who escorts them around, appears friendly and open. As they listen to the providers interacting with the children, they hear frequent examples of the children talking and the providers expanding on the children's sentences. They also see instances of the providers encouraging the children to interact with one another. Finally, Claire's mother noticed that one little boy was difficult to understand because his speech was "mushy." The provider interacting with him always tried to acknowledge what he said, repeating what he said using a correct speech model, but never asking him to repeat her.

What should Claire's parents do? Well, if you are like us, we would suggest that they sign Claire up now! This particular setting, given the information provided, appears ideal. There appear to be knowledgeable and caring providers, who are interested in continuing their understanding of child development. The amount of attention the providers can offer to the children seems appropriate, given the number of providers and children. There seem to be opportunities for both child-initiated and adult-guided learning. The providers are expanding on the children's sentences, which should help the children increase their length of sentences and the topics they can discuss. In essence, this seems to be the total package in childcare. What else could a parent want?!

What Type of Childcare Is Best for My Preschooler?

Lee is a single father raising twin boys, ages four-and-a-half. His job allows him to work out of his home, enabling him to be with his sons every day. However, lately he has felt his sons need more interaction with other children and, perhaps, other adults, so he begins investigating local childcare situations. At one local facility, he is initially impressed. The literature for the program states that all "teachers" have a minimum of a college degree, and all have some specialization in child development. The program boasts of its academic program, reporting that most of the "students" graduate from the program and go into a local prestigious, private elementary school that is notoriously selective. As he looks around the classroom for the four-year-olds, he sees respectful children sitting in chairs around small tables. They are filling in papers dealing with their ABCs. At one point, he hears a teacher call on one child, who recites the alphabet and then counts to 100!

Further observation of the school reveals a large section devoted to books. Children check these books out, along with cassette tapes, and listen to them via headphones. A chart documents all the books each child has completed. A schedule of events on the bulletin board reveals that a typical day involves circle time, focusing on weather and calendar study, math time, reading time, exercise, lunch, nap, and then free choice (math, reading, or writing). All providers in the program are very well groomed and polite.

How would you advise Lee about this facility? We would advise Lee to turn around and walk away! This program, though well meaning, has several significant characteristics that do not match what we know about language development and childcare. First, although the "teachers" are well educated, it appears their intent is to provide care against what we know to be best practices for preschool children. Remember, as we said earlier, preschoolers are active learners and explorers who should be guided, not directed, in their learning. These providers are not following the children's lead; rather, they are dictating what the children should do. In addition, they are assuming reading and other academic areas should be taught at this age. As you know, children can learn a great deal about literacy at this stage of development, but that learning should be accomplished through natural, engaging, and entertaining everyday activities. Asking children to sit down and memorize certain concepts does not help them acquire skills any faster than other children. Plus, it may lead to a stifling of development, because the children resent not being able to explore and learn on their own. Finally, even though the program encourages literacy through books, it relies on cassette tapes to do the "teaching." Thus, even though the children are hearing books being read, there are no opportunities for them to interact with others about the books' content or to learn the functions of books, words, or print.

In essence, it seems that this program has lost sight of the fact that these children are preschoolers, not high-school students! Lee's sons can do much better at a different site that follows what you know about language development and best practices in childcare.

Chapter Summary

FINDING A CHILDCARE situation for your child is not an easy task, as you might imagine. However, we have found that the more informed parents are as they begin choosing a place for their child, the more successful the outcome.

The four scenarios we presented represent real childcare situations. The experiences these parents had in their pursuit of an appropriate childcare program are not unique. What perhaps *may* be unique is that all of these parents did the right thing: They investigated each program. They observed and they asked questions. This approach to finding a childcare placement for your child is crucial. By observing and asking questions, you have a better chance finding the right place. And after all, isn't that the objective of all parents who find it necessary to use childcare? We want our children to be safe, happy, learning, and developing. We know you have the tools to be knowledgeable judges of childcare. Good luck on this important decision. May the best childcare win!

9

When You Suspect a Language Delay: Getting Help

DID YOU KNOW?

- Hearing loss can be temporary or permanent.
- Children with mental retardation often make significant advances in their speech and language development.
- Parents concerned about their child's speech and language skills should seek the help of a certified speech-language pathologist.

A few years ago, we had the opportunity to collaborate on a case involving a four-year-old boy. We had recently begun working in a university training program when one of the supervisors approached us about Joe. "I don't know what to do about Joe. I have tried everything I can think of and he is still almost unintelligible. His parents, Barbara and David, are concerned about his lack of progress in speech therapy, and now his pediatrician is suggesting that they go elsewhere for services."

Well, we reacted positively to several things the supervisor told us. First, Joe's parents obviously placed a high priority on speech and wanted the very best services for their son. Second, Joe's pediatrician was not content to simply hope for the best, to see if he would "grow out of this problem." These factors indicated strong outside support for Joe and his communication skills. Third, we were excited about the challenge. We wondered whether there might be something particularly unique about Joe's speech development. As it turns out, there was! Joe said *tan* for *can*, yet pronounced other *k* or *g* sounds correctly, like *coke* and *goose*. Joe also said *ko* for *toe*, yet pronounced *tea* correctly! This confusion between the *k* and *t* sounds appeared at first to be random. However, when we looked closer, we found that it was not random at all.

Joe's choice of sounds was dependent upon the vowel that followed them. The *o* and *u* sounds are made in the back of the mouth and so is the *k*, so Joe could say those together. On the other hand, the *ee* and *a* sounds are made in the front of the mouth and so is the *t*, so Joe would say those together. It was mixing the vowels in the back of the mouth with consonants in the front of the mouth (or vice versa) that was tricky for Joe. Once we discovered this, we set up our treatment activities to help Joe pronounce words like *cat, keep,* and *get* as well as words like *tooth, do,* and *dough*. He soon made great progress in treatment.

When You Have Questions

AFTER READING THE first eight chapters of this book, we hope you have a good working knowledge of how your child is acquiring her speech and language skills and the factors that influence her development. We have written this book so you can be filled with the same joy and awe we have experienced with our children and that we continue to experience as we learn and teach about this fascinating subject. However, because of our experiences as language specialists and as parents ourselves, we know that parents may have concerns about their child's language skills and desire specific, professional advice.

In this chapter, we provide some information on possible causes for language problems in children. Within each section, we provide a brief overview of the problem and suggestions for what to do about your concerns. As you will see, the professional most likely to be involved is the speech-language pathologist. Speech-language pathologists have specific knowledge in the areas of language development and the procedures used to determine whether a language delay exists and what should be done if a problem is found. To become a certified speech-language pathologist, an individual must complete a graduate degree. During the graduate program, our students log hundreds of hours of supervised experiences working with a variety of individuals with communication disorders. As a result, you can be confident that consulting with a certified speech-language pathologist is a good place to begin should you have concerns about your child's language development.

> Speech-language pathologists have specific knowledge in the areas of language development and the procedures used to determine whether a language delay exists and what should be done if a problem is found.

Depending on the setting to which parents take their concerns, they may see other professionals in addition to speech-language pathologists. If the parents are seeking help in a medical setting, there is a good chance that the insurance company will require them to first see their child's pediatrician. If the parents are seeking help through the local school system, their child's classroom teacher will be involved as well as other professionals such as the school psychologist. Regardless of the situation, though, the speech-language pathologist is the professional most qualified to determine whether a language problem exists.

Chances are you won't need the information contained in this chapter. However, statistically, we know that approximately 5 to 10 percent of all children struggle to some extent in learning language. We encourage you to read the following information carefully, and if some of the information seems to characterize your child's language skills, consult a speech-language pathologist. If the diagnosis confirms your concerns, keep in mind what we said in the introduction: Early intervention can make a world of positive difference to your child.

Possible Causes of Language Delay

WE SEE MANY children: infants, babies, toddlers, preschoolers, and even school-age children who are struggling with one or more areas of language development. Some of these children are having a difficult time in the area of phonology, showing signs of problems learning to produce speech sounds. These are children who continue to be difficult to understand beyond the age you would expect. Other children may have problems in the areas of semantics or morphology. These children are slow to develop new words, word endings (such as -ing, or -ed), smaller "functional" words (such as is, am, or was), or complex, multiword sentences. Other children may be struggling with how to use their language to get their needs met. For example, some children may not know how to ask for objects or actions they want. Finally, some children experience problems in more than one of these areas.

What is causing these problems in development? As we often say to parents who ask us this question, if we could provide a definitive answer to this question every time it is asked, we would both be millionaires! Unfortunately, at this point we often do not know why many children with language-learning problems struggle in their development. For some children, the cause is a bit more obvious. They may have other conditions that lead to language problems, such as hearing loss, mental retardation, autism, and so on. We will begin our discussion about these conditions first. However, for many children with language delays, the cause of the problem is unknown. Thus, we conclude this section on possible language delays with information on "specific language impairment."

Hearing Loss

Missy and Ron were worried about their two-year-old son and brought him to a speech, language, and hearing clinic for an evaluation. Although Michael was two, he was not using any meaningful words. Instead, he babbled some, gestured some, and screamed to let his parents know when he wanted something or was unhappy. During the evaluation involving a number of professionals, the speech-language pathologist noticed that Michael looked her in the eye, smiled consistently, and used gestures and pointing to indicate that he wanted toys in the room. When his hearing was tested, the team of professionals discovered he had a significant hearing loss.

Although Missy and Ron were frightened and worried at first, they worked with the professionals to develop a plan of treatment that the parents and team felt best met Michael's needs. Over time,

Michael responded well to a speech and language treatment involving sign and spoken language. Through the help of the team members, Missy and Ron became quite proficient in sign language and the strategies they could use at home to encourage Michael's speech and language development.

Michael's hearing loss was preventing him from learning spoken language. In fact, there are two different types of hearing loss, one of which is more severe than the other. A conductive hearing loss is one in which sound is having a difficult time reaching the inner ear, that part of the hearing system that sends the message to the brain. Typically, a conductive loss means that there is either something blocking the sound from getting to the eardrum (for example, a heavy buildup of wax or some "foreign" object), or something causing the middle ear bones not to move (in most cases, this may be fluid buildup from ear infections). Typically, simply removing the obstruction or decreasing the fluid in the middle ear can fix this kind of hearing loss. Thus, conductive hearing losses can be temporary.

A second type of hearing loss is called a sensorineural hearing loss. This is the type of hearing loss Michael had. With this type, there is a problem either with the inner ear itself or with the transfer of messages from the inner ear to the brain. This is more difficult to fix because it is a permanent hearing loss. Children with sensorineural loss are usually helped with one or more compensatory measures. These measures include the use of hearing aids to amplify the sounds the children hear, the surgical implantation of a cochlear device to take the place of the part of the inner ear that is not working, or the use of another communication system, such as sign language.

As you probably already know, hearing loss can affect spoken language development. However, the manner and extent to which language development will be affected varies from child to child. Much of this effect depends on the *type* of loss it is (conductive or sensorineural), how *severe* the hearing loss is, and *when* the hearing loss begins.

The severity of a hearing loss can range from a mild loss that may minimally affect what the child hears and learns, to a severe loss, meaning the child is able to hear little if any of the spoken language around her. Thus, the more severe the hearing loss, the greater the chance that spoken language will be delayed.

The effects of a hearing loss also depend somewhat on when the loss begins. In general, the earlier the hearing loss begins, the greater the effects will be on spoken language development. If a child has acquired some language and then loses a significant amount of her hearing, she will have already developed some knowledge of how language works. Helen Keller is a good example of this phenomenon.

The more severe the hearing loss, the greater the chance that spoken language will be delayed.

However, if a child is born with a significant hearing loss, there is a good chance that she will miss out on the language models she needs early in life to develop spoken language in a typical manner.

We are not suggesting that children who are born with significant, sensorineural hearing loss cannot acquire *language*. In fact, studies show that children who are born with significant hearing loss and have parents who immediately begin communicating with them using a means other than spoken language, such as sign language, acquire language in a similar rate and manner as those children who are learning spoken language. Unfortunately, this scenario is fairly rare; parents are not expecting their child to have a hearing loss. By the time the child is identified as having a hearing loss, and some measures are taken to help that child have access to language (the parents learn sign language, the child is given hearing aids, and so forth), a great deal of valuable time has elapsed. With the recent passage of federal legislation requiring that hearing be screened in newborn babies, we expect this situation will change. The most important point is to ensure that treatment begins as soon as a hearing loss is identified so that the child can quickly receive consistent and constant language models.

What Should Parents Do If They Suspect a Hearing Loss?

So, what are parents to do if they think that their child cannot hear or does not hear well? Most likely the first step is to consult their pediatrician with their concerns. Parents should be ready to provide specific examples of behaviors that suggest to them that their child is not responding, or responding well, to sounds. For example, it may be that the parents have noted that their child does not turn to the sound of his parents' voices or does not startle when pots are dropped on the floor. The more descriptive the parents are in their concerns, the clearer the picture for the pediatrician.

A wise pediatrician will take the parents' concerns seriously and likely do one or more tests. It may be that the pediatrician will first rule out that the child does not have a conductive hearing loss by examining the child's ear canal and eardrum and performing a test called tympanometry. This test will allow the physician to determine whether your child's middle ear area is working well or not, perhaps because of a buildup of fluid. The doctor next will likely order an assessment of the child's hearing.

Professionals who are highly qualified to test individuals' hearing are called audiologists. An audiologist determines how well an individual responds to sounds of varying types and loudness levels. This kind of testing, called audiometric testing, can provide a good picture of a child's hearing capabilities. The audiologist also may be the professional who conducts the typmanometry testing.

If a child's hearing is not within typical limits, then the family and the professionals involved will need to jointly decide the course of action. Decisions may need to be made about the use of other communication systems, such as sign language, and the use of assistive devices, such as hearing aids. There are many materials and resources that parents can obtain to help them in those decisions, and we've listed some of these at the end of this chapter. In the meantime, it is important to keep in mind what we said earlier in this section. *The child needs to have consistent and constant language models provided to him as soon as possible!* This will help the child to learn language in a more timely and efficient manner.

Mental Retardation

It seems that this is the diagnosis parents consider most frequently when their children are not learning language at the typical rate. Children with mental retardation, often referred to as children who are mentally challenged or children with developmental disabilities, experience problems with the activities that occur daily. One of these activities is communication, or using and understanding language. Other activities include dressing oneself, caring for oneself, using gross and fine motor movements to play or conduct daily actions, and so on. Children with mental retardation may be slower to develop in one or more of these areas.

Common types of mental retardation include Down syndrome and Fragile X syndrome, although there are many other types of mental retardation as well. Both of these syndromes involve abnormalities in the child's chromosomes. Even though these two types of mental retardation can be traced back to the child's genetic makeup, the cause for these occurrences, and of other types of mental retardation, is often not known. We have worked with parents who feel *they have caused* their child's mental retardation. Except in cases involving physical child abuse by the parent, the chance that a parent actually caused the mental retardation is extremely low.

Children can vary in the extent of their mental retardation. Some children are mildly affected; others are affected to a much more significant degree. As a general rule, the more severe the mental retardation, the greater the effect on language development. It is important, though, not to assume that a child with mental retardation has just a "fixed" amount of capabilities to learn language. Unfortunately, some individuals, including some professionals, assume that a child is able to develop language only to a certain extent when she has the label of mental retardation. They feel that children learn language to a level that is commensurate with their I.Q. However, scientific studies do not support this assumption. Researchers have shown that children who have scored low on tests of intelligence are able to make gains in language development that would not have been predicted given their supposed I.Q. Thus, one should never assume that a child with mental retardation will be limited in her capabilities based on some preconceived stereotype. It is important that all children with mental retardation receive services to allow them to communicate to the fullest extent of their capabilities. The best way to determine a child's capabilities is, in reality, by providing specific and individualized intervention and monitoring her progress in language development.

> We have worked with parents who feel *they have caused* their child's mental retardation. The chance that a parent actually caused the mental retardation is extremely low.

What Should Parents Do If They Suspect Mental Retardation?

For the most part, parents of children with Down syndrome will know their child has this form of mental retardation almost immediately. The facial characteristics are typically visible at birth or shortly thereafter. This was true for the Carters, a couple who had three children. When their third daughter, April, was born, they were told she had Down syndrome. However, if it is not until later that some parents suspect their child might have a form of mental retardation, they should seek professional advice by going to their pediatrician or their local school. It is likely that the pediatrician or special education professional for their school district will consult a number of different professionals, including a developmental or educational psychologist and a speech-language pathologist. An audiologist will probably be involved, because children with Down syndrome or other forms of mental retardation often have frequent ear infections as well. In the case of the Carter family, April often had ear infections, resulting in conductive, or temporary, significant hearing loss. April received antibiotics for the infections and special attention was given to making communication clearer when the adults around her knew she was not hearing as well.

To determine whether a child has mental retardation, and to what extent it exists, testing will involve descriptions and observations of the child's basic skills. The testing will be conducted to determine the child's language, cognitive, social, motor, and other common, functional skills. Parents should be ready to provide descriptions of what their child can do on her own and what she can do with some help or guidance from her parents. This type of information is crucial to determining the child's capabilities and is often not available when children are formally tested outside of their everyday, life experiences. Whenever parents are reporting what their child can do, it is important (though sometimes difficult) to be as descriptive and objective as possible. It will not be helpful to the professional or the child to over- or under-estimate the child's skills.

When a child is diagnosed with mental retardation, it may be that the professionals and family will determine that an additional communication system, such as sign language or picture boards, should be used to supplement the learning of spoken language. These alternative means of communicating have been shown to be a type of bridge or guide to helping children with mental retardation to learn spoken language. Parents must keep in mind what we said earlier: It is difficult to determine a child's potential in language development by just knowing that she has mental retardation. Parents should advocate for their child if some professionals take the stance that children with mental retardation are automatically limited to a prescribed degree. On the other hand, they should also be open to options that professionals offer that focus on increasing their child's capabilities.

> Parents must keep in mind that it is difficult to determine a child's potential in language development by just knowing that she has mental retardation.

April Carter's speech-language pathologist used sign language as part of the language development treatment plan she implemented, and she helped April's parents learn sign language too. In April's case, sign language seemed to help her begin to use spoken language. Soon, April was using spoken words more than signs. When this happened, the sign language use was faded out and April was encouraged to build up and refine the speech and language skills she was developing.

Autism

Parents may have some specific ideas about what autism is. Because of popular movies such as *Rain Man,* there is a media view of autism that is somewhat narrow. Many people assume that individuals with autism are somewhat "antisocial" yet have excellent memory skills for what seems to be unimportant information. Children with autism, or more specifically and accurately, autism spectrum disorder, demonstrate a wide range of abilities and behaviors that fall under this very general heading. Autism spectrum disorder is characterized by one or more of the following: delayed language development; unusual speech rhythms; high levels of exact imitations of others' language; decreased social interactions; lack of emotional contact with others and poor friendship-building; sensitivity, or lack of sensitivity, to touch; repetitiveness in language and actions; preoccupation with certain actions or objects; and a desire for "sameness" in surroundings. The degrees to which these characteristics are demonstrated and the number that are present vary considerably among children with autism spectrum disorder.

As the name suggests, autism spectrum disorder represents a whole spectrum, or continuum, of disabilities. For example, one condition that falls within the autism spectrum disorder is called Asperger's Syndrome. This particular syndrome may not be as obvious as other forms of autism spectrum disorder in that the child with Asperger's Syndrome has a much milder form of language impairment and may not demonstrate some of the more common characteristics of autism. The term pervasive developmental disorder also is associated with autism spectrum disorder. This term is used at times as a diagnostic label for young children who have problems in many different developmental areas, with characteristics similar to those of autism.

The cause of autism spectrum disorder is unknown. Unfortunately, when autism spectrum disorder was first discussed, some researchers erroneously thought that the disability was due to "cold mothers." In other words, they thought that the children were reacting to nonnurturing mothers. Today, we know this to be untrue. Causes have been speculated, ranging from chemical imbalances in the brain to toxins in the environment to disturbances in diets. In reality, the exact cause is unknown at this point. What is known is that autism spectrum disorder has its onset early in development, within the first three years of life. Parents often report that their child appeared to be developing appropriately and then "something happened." The child suddenly stopped talking or started developing some of the characteristics mentioned. Should this occur, parents are urged to consult a professional to determine the cause of this disruption in language development and the appropriate means of intervention.

What Should Parents Do If They Suspect Autism?

Judy and Steve were concerned about their four-year-old son. He could spend hours lining up his cars into different rows. He rarely said anything, and when he did, it was a rather high-pitched squeal. Family members suggested that perhaps Judy and Steve were talking too much for their son. However, Judy had other thoughts. When she was a teenager, she had volunteered at a neighbor's house, working with a young boy with autism. Both Judy and Steve were quite worried but had no idea who to ask for help.

Because some of the hallmark characteristics of autism spectrum disorder are a lack of language development and an underdeveloped intent to communicate, it may not be until the child is two or three that parents become sufficiently concerned to seek professional consultation. Again, depending on the setting they choose, they may consult their pediatrician or the local school district. In either case, the professional in charge will likely assemble a team of experts, including a speech-language pathologist, a physician, a developmental psychologist, and possibly a special-education teacher with expertise in autism spectrum disorder. Much of the testing will involve descriptions of the child's skills that come from observations and parent reports. Just as we have mentioned in earlier sections, parents' reports will be crucial to developing a complete and accurate picture of the child's capabilities.

Once a child has been diagnosed with autism spectrum disorder, the family and the professionals involved will need to make some specific decisions as to how to help the child develop his language and social skills. Some decisions will include whether an additional communication system should be used (sign language, picture systems that represent language) and what type of intervention or teaching the child should receive. Some professionals may advocate for instructional programs that have a strict behavioral modification approach underlying them. In these programs, children are taught language by strict imitation and "stimulus-response" techniques. Other professionals may suggest programs that emphasize creating a need for the child to communicate, with active and consistent modeling by the adults. Some programs may fall somewhere in the middle of these. Parents of children with autism spectrum disorder will need to educate themselves on the rationale for these different types of programs, the research that supports their use, and how children's language skills have changed based on these programs.

Regarding this last point, it will be particularly important that parents determine how the professionals measure language and whether they look at how children communicate in real-life, everyday situations. Although improvement on specific tests might seem impressive, the important issue is whether the treatment is resulting in an increase in the way that the child communicates with those around him in daily, natural situations. Once again, the important point is that professionals should use strategies that help children communicate in a meaningful way with those in their environment. Likewise, parents should make every attempt to ensure that true communication is the ultimate goal and that the professionals are working with them, as well as their child, on the development of the best strategies for communication.

> Professionals should use strategies that help children communicate in a meaningful way with those in their environment.

In the case of Judy and Steve, they received help from their local school district. A team of professionals helped evaluate their son and decide on a treatment plan. He indeed had autism, and the team developed a system of communication that emphasized ways the young boy could communicate using signs and pictures. As the months progressed, Judy and Steve began to see some progress in their son's communication development. Though they knew it would be a lifelong process, they felt relieved that they were able to participate in helping their son develop to his fullest potential.

Specific Speech or Language Impairment: Delay of Unknown Origin

Heather and James brought their daughter, Joy, to a university-based speech, language, and hearing clinic when she was three years old. Both were faculty members at the university. Joy was speaking in one- and two-word sentences. Because Joy's older sister, Renee, had begun talking early and quickly progressed in her language skills, they wondered whether they were expecting too much from Joy. They wanted to allow Joy to develop at her own pace, but also were worried that they should be doing more to help Joy develop her language skills faster. The speech, language, and hearing evaluation confirmed that Joy's language skills were below what was expected for her age.

Based on typical language development, the speech-language pathologist established specific goals for Joy. For example, she needed to use a greater variety of two-word sentences and increase the frequency of certain types of three-word sentences. At the same time, Heather and James were guided in how to model these specific language skills at home. Both parents had inadvertently decreased their own communication with Joy because of her lack of responsiveness. In subsequent sessions with the speech-language pathologist, Heather and James happily reported that they were using the new strategies at home, even when it seemed Joy did not respond the way they expected. Joy made wonderful progress in treatment, and by the time she started school, her spoken language was similar to the other children. The speech-language pathologist then provided Heather and James with specific suggestions for increasing Joy's opportunities to learn about written language through language play and reading experiences.

> Children with a history of language or learning delays in their family are prone to language problems, but that does not necessarily mean that those children will have a language delay.

For many children like Joy, the cause of a speech or language impairment remains a mystery. They may not be learning the speech sounds correctly, so that their speech is highly difficult to understand. They may be experiencing difficulties linking words and word endings together, such that their sentences appear immature for their age. No matter the type of language problem, it seems unrelated to their ability to hear, their mental capabilities, or any autistic-like tendencies. In cases like this, children are labeled as having a specific language impairment.

Researchers have tried to determine whether common childhood illnesses, such as recurring ear infections, may be the culprits in specific language impairments. At this point, there is nothing to suggest that constant ear infections always lead to language problems. While infections and fluid in a child's ear do not help the child hear his parents' language models well, it usually is only a temporary, conductive hearing loss. Thus, this cannot be a "pat answer" to why a child is not learning language in the typical manner.

Other researchers, and many parents, have wondered whether language problems are related to language delays that parents or other close relatives have experienced. This is definitely a possibility. Research has shown that at least for some children with language problems, there *is* a genetic component to the delay. Children whose parents struggled learning to talk or to read and write are more apt to have a language problem. Note how we have written this, though. Children with a history of language or learning delays in their family are prone to language problems, but that does not necessarily mean that those children *will* have a language delay. Again, it is difficult to determine just who will have a language delay.

> The child begins with an idea to communicate, which her system must translate into the appropriate speech sounds, words, and type of sentence structure to use.

Ultimately, for children with language delays of unknown origins, or children with specific language impairment, we typically explain to parents that the "wiring" in their child's brain that is used to learn language is not helping the child to the extent it needs to. We know this for sure: Language is in the brain. That is where we understand language and make the commands to produce it. Just as some of us are born with wiring that is less than efficient in helping us learn to do certain athletic moves, sing, or calculate difficult math problems, some children are born with wiring that is less efficient for helping them learn language. As our medical technology becomes more sophisticated, there will likely come a day when we can be more specific about what seems to be going awry.

In the meantime, it is important for parents not to panic when they hear discussions about language in the brain and wiring that isn't helping their child learn language in a timely manner. When a child is language delayed, it means that she will require special input and models to help that wiring accomplish the task that needs to be done: to learn language.

What Should Parents Do If They Suspect a Specific Language Impairment?

When parents note that their child is not developing language as outlined in chapters 1 through 4 of this book, they should take their concerns to a local speech-language pathologist. Again, it may be that they must do this via their pediatrician or local school district. Specific examples of what their child's speech, vocabulary, sentence structure, social language abilities, and other developing language skills are like will prove to be invaluable in helping the speech-language pathologist determine whether the child has a specific language impairment. The speech-language pathologist will likely take this information and, together with information obtained from observations of the child and test results, determine a diagnosis. If the diagnosis is for specific language impairment, then suggestions for intervention to improve the child's language skills will be provided.

Speech-language pathologists use many of the principles that we discussed in the first few chapters to facilitate language acquisition in children with specific language impairment. The speech-language pathologist will set goals for specific language skills based on what is known about the sequence of typical language development. Situations in which the specific language skills naturally occur will be used in treatment. The speech-language pathologist will follow the child's interests and model the language skills frequently. She also will give the child many opportunities to use the new skills in a meaningful way that fits the communication demands of the situation.

There are other specific causes for language delay that are beyond the scope of this book. The resources we provide at the end of this chapter should help you learn more about other causes. It is important to know, though, that for many children with language problems, the exact cause will always remain uncertain.

Other Problems Associated with Language Delays

CHILDREN WHO ARE struggling to learn language, as well as children who are learning language in a typical fashion, sometimes have accompanying problems that may or may not be related to language development abilities. Two such problems are stuttering and attention deficit disorder.

Stuttering

As children are learning to talk, they invariably experience moments when their speech is anything but fluent. It is not uncommon to hear a young child of three repeat the first word of a sentence over and over again. When Nick was three-and-a-half, he decided to announce to his parents, his grandparents, and a whole slew of relatives his recent accomplishment. It sounded something like this:

"My-my-my-my-my-my-my-my-my-my-my car won!"

Of course, all of Nick's relatives turned to his father with a look like, "Well, what are you going to do about *that?!*" Fortunately, being a student of child language development, Nick's father knew that this type of repetition was completely typical and even somewhat expected for children Nick's age.

When children are developing language, they have an incredible number of different tasks to perform simultaneously. The child begins with an idea to communicate, which her system must translate into the appropriate speech sounds, words, and type of sentence structure to use. Not only are the sounds, words, and sentence types new and challenging for the child, but she usually chooses to communicate while also engaged in a very exciting, playful activity. It is no wonder that children sometimes end up overloading the system, resulting in nonfluent speech. These "nonfluencies" often are characterized by repetitions of whole words and phrases, or even parts of words *(dog-dog-dog-doghouse)*. Typically developing children may do this as much as one out of every ten words. When these symptoms occur, parents should consider them to be typical aspects of language development.

However, there are times when children begin to show nonfluent speech that is different from the typical examples found in language development. In these cases, a child may begin to repeat just the sounds of a word *(b-b-b-b-boy)* or perhaps prolong one sound over a period of time *(sssssssssister)*. The child also might show some kind of facial tension or grimace. Finally, it may be that the child produces any type of repetition or prolongation quite often (that is, on more than one out of every ten words). These types of "dysfluencies" are considered to be out of the typical realm and *may* indicate a stuttering condition. If these occur over a period of a month, the parents should have the child evaluated by a speech-language pathologist.

Whether the child is producing typical nonfluencies or nontypical dysfluencies, one of the best approaches for parents to take is to allow the child to finish his communication. It is so easy for a parent to want to finish the child's sentence for him. However, that will not help the child produce more fluent speech. In addition, parents also can model easy, slower, less complex speech for their children. This does not mean parents should talk so slowly that the typical person falls asleep! It means that parents can break their normally complex sentences ("We need to stop by the grocery store because we have the party that is for your grandmother who is turning 65 coming up.") into smaller, less complex sentences with pauses at appropriate places ("We need to stop at the grocery store. (pause) Remember, we're having a party for Grandma. (pause) She's going to be 65 years old."). By modifying their speech rate and showing patience for their child's speech rate and fluency, parents can provide the help their child might need to become more fluent.

Attention Deficit Hyperactive Disorder With or Without Hyperactivity

In the last decade, perhaps no other disabilities have received so much attention, and been so highly diagnosed, as attention deficit disorders, with or without hyperactivity (ADD/ADHD). Children with ADD/ADHD are said to suffer from an inability or poor ability to attend to or concentrate on the topic at hand. They are characterized as distractible and impulsive. Up to two-thirds of children with ADD/ADHD also have a language delay.

ADD/ADHD is a controversial diagnosis. Specific, definable, and consistent criteria for this diagnosis, that discriminate this disorder from others, are not used. That is, the criteria used by one professional to diagnose a child with ADD/ADHD may not be the same collection of behaviors used by another professional to diagnose another child. There is concern that some of the behaviors attributed to ADD/ ADHD may be just typical behaviors in young children. Additionally, many children with the ADD/ADHD label are able to maintain attention and concentrate in some situations (playing games) even though they cannot in other situations (structured activities requiring specific language skills, such as reading). Adding to the controversy is that many if not most children with ADD/ADHD are prescribed medications that have not been examined for their long-term effects on humans.

Adding to the controversy is that many if not most children with ADD/ADHD are prescribed medications that have not been examined for their long-term effects on humans.

When parents suspect their child has ADD/ADHD, or a professional suggests this to the parents, they would be well advised to educate themselves on all aspects of this disorder, including what research supports the label, any new research about the long-term effects of medication on children, and nonmedicinal interventions that can be used. We also urge parents to consider having their child's language abilities evaluated in depth to determine whether other possible factors, such as language delay, may be leading to the symptoms identified as ADD/ADHD. Even when parents and professionals determine that a medicinal course of action is warranted, services to help the child learn how to best use his abilities to attend, listen, and so forth, should be considered.

Implications of Language Delay for Later Learning

IT IS IMPORTANT to know that children who experience difficulties learning to use language in the first five years of life are at risk for having difficulties in learning to read and write. Reading and writing are language skills. Like talking and listening, they are ways to communicate with others. Reading and writing tap into the areas of semantics, phonology, morphology, syntax, and pragmatics, just as talking and listening do. However, unlike talking and listening, reading and writing require children to *actively think* about the language system. Children who have had a difficult time learning the rules of language may have an additional struggle when they then have to think about the rules of language to read and write.

This does not mean all children who are delayed in spoken language will be delayed in written language. It does mean, however, that parents of children with delayed language development should be encouraging their child's early literacy skills and observant of their children's reading and writing abilities as they enter formal schooling. In chapter 4, we provided some examples of what parents could do at home to encourage their child's written language abilities. Parents could use these activities to be proactive in developing their children's literacy skills. We also would suggest that parents of children with language problems notify the child's teachers to be aware of any special help the child might need as she learns to read and write.

The bottom line for concerned parents is to be persistent in seeking help for their child and to be the child's best advocate. If any professional with whom a parent consults does not seem to discuss language development in the manner in which it

has been discussed in this book, consider consulting with another professional. In our experiences, children whose parents have learned as much as they can about language development and have been actively involved in the evaluation and interventionprocesses are the

children who have made some of the best progress in their language skills.

Where Do Parents Find Help?

NO MATTER THE cause of the language problem, parents must seek help from the appropriate professional. As we have stated, the speech-language pathologist is typically involved directly as the main professional conducting an evaluation or as part of a professional team. Some speech-language pathologists work with a pediatrician or school system, and thus can be contacted via either professional source. Others work in private practices and can be contacted directly through a local directory.

Parents will, of course, want to seek services from a qualified professional. They should look for specific credentials when selecting a speech-language pathologist. Optimally, the speech-language pathologist should be certified by the American Speech-Language-Hearing Association (ASHA). This is the national association for over 100,000 speech-language pathologists and audiologists. This organization, which has been in existence for over 75 years, is dedicated to helping speech-language pathologists help children and adults and their families with communication disorders. ASHA certification is indicated by the letters "CCC-SLP" after the professional's name (for example, Kenn Apel, Ph.D., CCC-SLP). Professional credentials are also administered at the state level. Many states require that speech-language pathologists be licensed to practice. Finally, school districts usually require that speech-language pathologists be certified. The educational requirements for ASHA certification, state licensure, and school certification often are similar. Most require a graduate degree and appropriate clinical training.

When an evaluation is conducted, the speech-language pathologist and the other professionals involved will determine whether a language delay exists, possible causes for the delay, what skills the child uses on her own and with the aid of helping adults, what skills she needs to learn, and what strategies might best work with her. The prognosis for improvement, or the likelihood for further developing her language skills, also will be discussed. Should the speech-language pathologist and other members of a team decide that the child requires intervention, or help, to improve her language skills, then a direct plan or set of goals will be established for how to best accomplish this task.

Just as in other professional areas, there are slight differences in how specific professionals intervene. For young children, we

206 ♦ WHEN YOU SUSPECT A LANGUAGE DELAY

generally advocate for intervention that promotes language development in situations or activities where real communication is occurring, rather than asking a child to imitate language for imitation's sake. In this latter situation, the adult is not helping the child understand *why* he is saying what he is saying.

We also believe in early intervention. That is, as soon as a child is diagnosed as having a language delay, no matter the cause, we suggest he receive language intervention. In some settings, this may not be possible. For example, in many school districts, federal or state laws mandate that school-based professionals can see only children who have disabilities that interfere with their education. If for some reason a child does not qualify for school-based services, or if parents want services provided by another professional, in addition to or instead of school services, this generally is possible.

In some communities, there may be a university that has a speech-language-hearing clinic associated with a graduate program in speech-language pathology. Some speech-language pathologists work out of local hospitals, developmental centers, specialized clinics, and Head Start Programs. Most pediatricians and local school districts should be aware of options for services in the area.

In addition to local sources, parents also may seek advice and information at the state and national levels. At the national level, parents can contact the American Speech-Language-Hearing Association (ASHA). ASHA has a number of publications for parents concerned about their child's language development. There is a toll-free number (1-800-638-8255) for concerned parents as well as a Web page (www.asha.org) that has information for parents and valuable links to other sites.

Finally, most states have state-level organizations representing speech-language pathologists and audiologists. Access numbers and Web sites can be obtained from the ASHA Web site.

Perhaps you are wondering about Joe, the young boy we discussed at the beginning of the chapter. Several years later, we saw Joe at a grocery store. He was a tall middle-school student, whose speech was quite good. In fact, had we not known Joe's history, we probably would not have guessed that he had struggled with speech so much as a preschool child.

Book Summary

WE HAVE PROVIDED you with information about how children develop language as well as the factors that may influence language development. We also have reviewed what might be some possible causes of language problems in children and what parents should do if they are concerned about their child's language skills. We hope this book has been both informative and interesting to you. Our real hope, though, is that you have come to understand as we do how language development is one of life's true miracles. Throughout the first five years of life, your child is acquiring a skill that serves as a foundation for almost every action and purpose he will undertake in life. We hope you have learned how important you are in this process and how completely enjoyable the process can be. We wish you luck as you engage in this fascinating area of child development. Enjoy it and have fun.

REFERENCES

Academy of Orton-Gillingham Practitioners and Educators. (2000). Retrieved September 22, 2000, from the World Wide Web: http://www.ols.net/users/orton/.

Ackerman-Ross, S., and P. Khanna. "The Relationship of High Quality Day Care to Middle-Class Three-Year-Olds' Language Performance." *Early Childhood Research Quarterly* 4 (1989): 97–116.

August, D., and K. Hakuta. *Improving Schooling for Language-Minority Children: A Research Agenda*. Washington, D.C.: National Academy Press, 1997.

Babrow, A. S., B. J. O'Keefe, D. L. Swanson, R. A. Meyers, and M. A. Murphy. "Person Perception and Children's Impressions of Television and Real Peers." *Communication Research* 15, no. 6 (1998): 680–698.

Barton, M. E., and R. Strosberg. "Conversational Patterns of Two-Year-Old Twins in Mother-Twin-Twin Triads." *Journal of Child Language* 24 (1997): 257–269.

Berk, L., and K. Krafft. "Private Speech in Two Preschools: Significance of Open-Ended Activities and Make-Believe Play for Verbal Self-Regulation." *Early Childhood Research Quarterly* 13, no. 4 (1998): 637–658.

Bilingual Therapies, Inc. (1999). Retrieved September 22, 2000, from the World Wide Web: http://www.bilingualtherapies.com.

Bishop, D.V.M. "Pre- and Perinatal Hazards and Family Background in Children with Specific Language Impairments: A Study of Twins." *Brain and Language* 56, no. 1 (1997): 1–26.

Bishop, D.V.M., and S. J. Bishop. "'Twin Language': A Risk Factor for Language Impairment?" *Journal of Speech, Language, and Hearing Research* 41, no. 1 (1998): 150–160.

Bock, R. (n.d.). "Why Children Succeed or Fail at Reading. Retrieved May 14, 2001 from the World Wide Web, National Institute of Child Health and Human Development: http://www.nichd.nih.gov/publications/pubs/readbro.htm.

Brownlee, S. (1998). "Baby Talk." Retrieved May 14, 2001, from the World Wide Web, U.S. News Online: http://www.usnews.com/usnews/issue/980615/15lang.htm.

Burchinal, M. R., J. E. Roberts, L. A. Nabors, and D. M. Bryant. "Quality of Center Child Care and Infant Cognitive and Language Development." *Child Psychology* 67 (1996): 606–620.

Cantor, J., and A. I. Nathanson. "Children's Fright Reactions to Television News." *Journal of Communication* 46, no. 4 (1996): 139–152.

Cervantes, C. A., and M. A. Callanan. "Labels and Explanations in Mother-Child Emotion Talk: Age and Gender Differentiation." *Developmental Psychology* 34, no. 1 (1998): 88–89.

Cochran, P.S. & Nelson, L.K. "Technology Applications in Intervention for Preschool-Age Children with Language Disorders." *Seminars in Speech and Language*, 20, no.3, (1999): 203-218.

Conti-Ramsden, G., G. D. Hutcheson, and J. Grove. "Contingency and Breakdown: Children with SLI and Their Conversations with Mothers and Fathers." *Journal of Speech and Hearing Research* 38 (1995): 1290–1302.

DeHouwer, A. (1999, July). Two or more languages in early childhood: Some general points and practical recommendations. *ERIC Clearinghouse on Languages and Linguistics Digest*. Retrieved May 14, 2001, from the World Wide Web: http://www.cal.org/ericcll/digest/earlychild.html.

Dodd, B., and S. McEvoy. "Twin Language or Phonological Disorder?" *Journal of Child Language* 21 (1994): 273–289.

Dunn, L., S. A. Beach, and S. Kontos. "Quality of the Literacy Environment in Day Care and Children's Development." *Journal of Research in Childhood Education* 9 (1994): 24–34.

Fitch, M., A. Huston, S. Piemyat, R. Truglio, and J. Wright. "Occupational Portrayals on Television: Career Aspirations and Perceptions of Reality." *Child Development* 66 (1995): 1706–1718.

Flavell, J. H., E. R. Flavell, F. L. Green, and J. E. Korfmacher. "Do Young Children Think of Television Images as Pictures or Real Objects?" *Journal of Broadcasting & Electronic Media* 34, no. 4 (1990): 399–419.

Fowler, W., K. Ogston, G. Roberts-Fiati, and A. Swenson. "The Effects of Enriching Language in Infancy on Early and Later Development of Competence." *Early Childhood Development and Care* 135 (1997): 41–77.

Frede, E. C. "The Role of Program Quality in Producing Early Childhood Program Benefits. *The Future of Children, 5*, no.3, (1995): 115-132. Retrieved May 14, 2001, from the World Wide Web:http://www.futureofchildren.org/lto/06_lto.htm

Gleason, J.B. *The Development of Language (5th Ed)*. Needham Heights, MA: Allyn & Bacon, (2000).

Goldberg, M. E., and G. J. Gorn. "Television's Impact on Preferences for Non-White Playmates: Canadian *Sesame Street* Inserts." *Journal of Broadcasting* 23, no. 1 (1979): 27–32.

Goodson, M. S., R. A. Hough, and J. R. Nurss. "Prereading/Language Development in Two Day Care Centers." *Journal of Reading Behavior* 13 (1981): 23–31.

Grossen, B. "A Synthesis of Research on Reading from the National Institute of the Child." *Health and Human Development.* (1997, November). Retrieved May 14, 2001, from the World Wide Web: http://www.nrrf.org/synthesis_research.htm.

Hanen Centre. (n.d.). Retrieved September 22, 2000, from the World Wide Web: http://www.hanen.org.

Hayes, D., S. Kelly, and M. Mandel. "Media Differences in Children's Story Synopses: Radio and Television Contrasted." *Journal of Educational Psychology* 78 (1986): 341–346.

Hoff-Ginsberg, E. "Older Siblings As Conversational Partners." *Merril-Palmer Quarterly* 37, no. 3 (1991): 465–482.

Hoff-Ginsberg, E. "The Relation of Birth Order and Socioeconomic Status to Children's Language Experience and Language Development." *Applied Psycholinguistics* 19, no. 4 (1998): 603–629.

Hoffner, C. J. Cantor, and E. Thorson. "Children's Understanding of a Televised Narrative." *Communication Research* 15, no. 3 (1988): 227–245.

Holloway, S. D., and M. Reichhart-Erickson. "The Relationship of Day Care Quality to Children's Free-Play Behavior and Social Problem-Solving Skills." *Early Childhood Research Quarterly* 3 (1988): 39–53.

Hopman-Rock, M., F. M. Gerritsen, and P. Talsma. "Socioeconomic Status and Gender Differences in Language Development of Children Aged 3 to 6 Years." *Pedagogische Studieen* 65, no. 11 (1988): 437–450.

I Am Your Child. (1997). Retrieved September 22, 2000, from the World Wide Web: http://www.iamyourchild.org/qualitycare /index.html.

James, N. C., and T. A. McCain. "Television Games Preschool Children Play: Patterns, Themes, and Uses." *Journal of Broadcasting* 26, no. 4 (1982): 783–800.

Kayser, H. G. *Assessment and Intervention Resource for Hispanic Children.* San Diego: Singular, 1998.

Kayser, H. G. *Bilingual Speech-Language Pathology: A Hispanic Focus.* San Diego: Singular, 1995.

Kontos, S. J. "Child Care Quality, Family Background, and Children's Development." *Early Childhood Research Quarterly* 6 (1991): 242–262.

Koutsouvanou, E. "Television and Child Language Development." *International Journal of Early Childhood* 25 (1993): 27–32.

Krafft, K. C., and L. E. Berk. "Private Speech in Two Preschools: Significance of Open-Ended Activities and Make-Believe Play for Verbal Self-Regulation." *Early Childhood Research Quarterly* 13, no. 4 (1998): 637–658.

Kunkel, D. "Children and Host-Selling Television Commercials." *Communication Research* 15, no. 1 (1988): 71–92.

Lahey, M. *Language Disorders and Language Development.* Needham, Mass.: Macmillan, 1988.

Lawton, J. T., and N. Fowell. "A Description of Teacher and Child Language in Two Preschool Programs." *Early Childhood Research Quarterly* 4 (1989): 407–432.

Lee, Y. A., J. S. Lee, and J. W. Lee. "The Role of the Play Environment in Young Children's Language Development." *Early Childhood Development and Care* 139 (1997): 49–71.

Macarthur Communicative Development Inventories. (2000). Retrieved September 22, 2000, from the World Wide Web: http://www.sci.sdsu.edu/cdi/

Marcon, R. A. "Differential Effects of Three Preschool Models on Inner-City 4-Year-Olds." *Early Childhood Research Quarterly* 7 (1992): 517–530.

Marvin, C. A., and A. J. Privratsky. "After-School Talk: The Effects of Materials Sent Home from Preschool." *American Journal of Speech-Language Pathology* 8 (1999): 231–240.

McCabe, A. E. "Differential Language Learning Styles in Young Children: The Importance of Context." *Developmental Review* 9, no. 1 (1989): 1–20.

McCartney, K. "Effect of Quality Day Care Environment on Children's Language Development." *Developmental Psychology* 20 (1984): 244–259.

,.

McKenna, W. M., and P. E. Ossoff. "Age Differences in Children's Comprehension of a Popular Television Program." *Child Study Journal* 28, no. 1 (1998): 53–68.

McLaughlin, S. *Introduction to Language Development.* San Diego: Singular, 1998.

McMahon, S., and B. Dodd. "A Comparison of the Expressive Communication Skills of Triplet, Twin and Singleton Children." *European Journal of Disorders of Communication* 32, no. 3 (1997): 328–345.

Medcalf-Davenport, N. A. "A Comparative Study of the General World Knowledge and Language Development of Pre-Kindergarten Children from Either Day Care or In-Home Care." *Early Childhood Development and Care* 93 (1993): 1–14.

Morra Pellegrino, M. L., and A. Scopesi. "Structure and Function of Baby Talk in a Day-Care Centre." *Journal of Child Language* 17 (1990): 101–114.

Morrow, L. M. "Young Children's Responses to One-to-One Story Readings in School Settings." *Reading Research Quarterly* 23, no. 1 (1988): 89–107.

National Reading Panel. (n.d.). Retrieved September 22, 2000, from the World Wide Web: http://www.nationalreadingpanel.org.

Nelson, L.K. & Masterson, J.J. "Computer Technology: Creative Interfaces in Service Delivery." *Topics in Language Disorders, 19,* no.3, (1999): 68-86.

Nelson, N. W. *Childhood Language Disorders in Context: Infancy Through Adolescence.* New York: Macmillan, 1993.

Nikken, P., and A. L. Peeters. "Children's Perceptions of Television Reality." *Journal of Broadcasting & Electronic Media* 32, no. 4 (1988): 441–452.

Oshima-Takane, Y., E. Goodz, and J. L. Derevensky. "Birth Order Effects on Early Language Development: Do Secondborn Children Learn from Overheard Speech?" *Child Development* 67 (1996): 621–634.

Owens, R. E., Jr. *Language Development: An Introduction.* 4th ed. Needham Heights, Mass.: Allyn & Bacon, 1996.

Paul, R. *Language Disorders from Infancy Through Adolescence: Assessment and Intervention.* St. Louis, Mo.: Mosby, 1995.

Pham, L. "Infant Dual Language Acquisition Revisited." *Journal of Educational Issues of Language Minority, 14,* (1994): 185-210. Retrieved September 27, 2001, from the World Wide Web: http://www.ncbe.gwu.edu/miscpubs/jeilms/vol14/pham.htm

Pine, J. M. "Variation in Vocabulary Development As a Function of Birth Order." *Child Development* 66 (1995): 272–281.

Polyzoi, E. "Quality of Young Children's Talk with Adult Caregivers and Peers During Play Interactions in the Day Care Setting." *Canadian Journal of Research in Early Childhood Education* 6 (1985): 21–30.

Rickard, C., and K. Younce. (2001). "Language Development." Retrieved May 14, 2001, from the World Wide Web: http://www .colorado.edu/slhs/SLHS4560.

Rodriguez, J. L., R. M. Diaz, D. Duran, and L. Espinosa. "The Impact of Bilingual Preschool Education on the Language Development of Spanish-Speaking Children." *Early Childhood Research Quarterly* 10 (1995): 475–490.

Schober-Peterson, D., and C. J. Johnson. "Non-Dialogue Speech During Preschool Interactions." *Journal of Child Language* 18 (1991): 153–170.

Segal, N. L., and T. D. Topoloski. "A Twin Research Perspective on Reading and Spelling Disabilities." *Reading and Writing Quarterly: Overcoming Learning Difficulties* 11, no. 2 (1995): 209–227.

Seinow, G. W., and E. P. Bettinghaus. "Television Exposure and Language Development." *Journal of Broadcasting* 26, no. 1 (1982): 470–479.

Senechal, M. "The Differential Effect of Storybook Reading on Preschoolers' Acquisition of Expressive and Receptive Vocabulary." *Journal of Child Language* 24 (1997): 123–138.

Short-Meyerson, K. J., and L. J. Abbeduto. "Preschoolers' Communication During Scripted Interactions." *Journal of Child Language* 24 (1997): 469–493.

Silverman, I. T., and J. N. Sprafkin. "The Effects of *Sesame Street*'s Prosocial Spots on Cooperative Play Between Young Children." *Journal of Broadcasting* 24, no. 2 (1980): 135–147.

Slobin, D. I., J. Gerhardt, A. Kyratzis, J. Guo. *Social Interaction, Social Context, and Language: Essays in Honor of Susan Ervin-Tripp.* Mahwah, N.J.: Lawrence Eribaum Associates, 1996.

Taylor, O. L., and L. B. Leonard. *Language Acquisition Across North America: Cross-Cultural and Cross-Linguistic Perspectives.* San Diego: Singular, 1999.

Thompson, R. B., and K. Moore. "Collaborative Speech in Dyadic Problem Solving: Evidence for Preschool Gender Differences in Early Pragmatic Development." *Journal of Language and Social Psychology* 19, no. 2 (2000): 248–255.

Tomblin, J. B. "The Effect of Birth Order on the Occurrence of Developmental Language Impairment." *British Journal of Disorders of Communication* 25 (1990): 77–84.

University of Massachussetts; Amherst: NIH Working Groups on AAE. (n.d.). Retrieved May 14, 2001, from the World Wide Web: http://www.umass.edu/aae/

Walker, K., and L. Armstrong. "Do Mothers and Fathers Interact Differently with Their Child or Is It the Situation Which Matters?" *Child: Care, Health & Development* 21, no. 3 (1995): 161–181.

Walma van der Molen, Juliette H., and Tom H. A. van der Voort. "Children's Recall of Television and Print News: A Media Comparison Study." *Journal of Educational Psychology* 89 (1997): 82–91.

Washington, J. A., and H. K. Craig. "Socioeconomic Status and Gender Influences on Children's Dialectical Variations." *Journal of Speech, Language, and Hearing Research* 41, no. 3 (1998): 618–626.

Westby, C. E., and R. Roman. "Finding the Balance: Learning to Live in Two Worlds." *Topics in Language Disorders* 15, no. 4 (1995): 68–88.

Winsler, A., R. M. Diaz, L. Espinosa, and J. L. Rodriguez. "When Learning a Second Language Does Not Mean Losing the First: Bilingual Language Development in Low-Income, Spanish-Speaking Children Attending Bilingual Preschool." *Child Development* 70, no. 2 (1999): 349–362.

Yamamoto, M. "Birth Order, Gender Differences, and Language Development in Modern Japanese Pre-School Children." *Psychologia: An International Journal of Psychology in the Orient* 33, no. 3 (1990): 185–190.

INDEX

ABOUT THE AUTHORS

Kenn Apel, Ph.D., CCC-SLP, is professor and chair of communication disorders and sciences at Wichita State University and a widely known educator and specialist in childhood language. He has over 20 years of experience working with children with speech and language disorders, has presented extensively across the country, and has published articles on the language and literacy skills of children and adolescents. He lives with his wife and daughter in Wichita, Kansas.

Julie J. Masterson, Ph.D., CCC-SLP, is a nationally known educator and specialist in child language development. She is professor of communication sciences and disorders at Southwest Missouri State University. Dr. Masterson has over 100 publications and presentations at professional conferences and has developed computer software for clinical use by language specialists. A frequent and popular speaker on the subject of child language development, she lives in Springfield, Missouri, with her husband, son, and daughter.

Help Your Child Discover the Joy of Learning

Does your child learn best in the morning, afternoon, or evening? Does his reading comprehension increase or decrease when music is played in the background? Does she prefer to study alone or with others? What works best for one child is often counterproductive for others. *Discover Your Child's Learning Style* shows you how to assess and nurture your child's individual learning potential based on his or her:

- **Talents**

- **Interests**

- **Disposition**

- **Preferred environment**

- **And much more!**

Inside is a step-by-step program of self-awareness tests that guide you to a better understanding of your child's unique strengths and weaknesses, goals and interests, and inner pace.

Includes "learning style" assessments for all ages

"Parents who understand the principles in this book will be better parents!"
—Richard and Linda Eyre, authors of *Teaching Your Children Values*

Discover Your Child's Learning Style

**Children Learn in Unique Ways—
Here's the Key to Every Child's
Learning Success**

Mariaemma Willis, M.S., and Victoria Kindle Hodson, M.A.

ISBN 0-7615-2013-9 / Paperback
352 pages / U.S. $19.95 / Can. $29.95

**To order, call (800) 632-8676 or
visit us online at www.primalifestyles.com**

P
PRIMA

Make a Difference During the Most Important Years of Your Child's Life

As a caring parent, you want to start your child out in life on the proper foundation. But where do you go for the answers to such questions as: How do I communicate with an infant who doesn't understand words? How can I effectively teach boundaries to my toddler? In this book you'll learn how to use kind but firm support to raise a child who is both capable and confident. You'll find practical solutions and solid advice on how to:

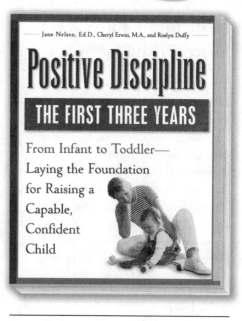

- **Encourage independence and exploration while providing appropriate boundaries**

- **Identify your child's temperament**

- **Understand what the latest research in brain development tells us about raising healthy children**

- **And much more!**

Containing real-life examples of challenges other parents and caregivers have faced, this book is the one book that no parent should be without.

ISBN 0-7615-1505-4 / Paperback
304 pages / U.S. $16.95 / Can. $25.95

P
PRIMA

**To order, call (800) 632-8676 or
visit us online at www.primalifestyles.com**

Discover How Music Can Improve Your Child's Mind

Recent scientific studies at some of the most respected universities in the world indicate that children introduced to classical music at a young age read earlier and perform better on achievement tests. In this book, respected educator Sharlene Habermeyer gives you a simple, step-by-step program that any parent can follow to harness the incredible power of music and bring out the best in your child. You'll discover how introducing children to good music can:

- **Accelerate language development**

- **Improve math and science skills**

- **Enhance physical coordination**

- **Strengthen memory and reading retention**

- **And more!**

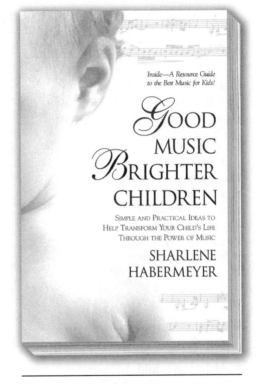

Inside—A Resource Guide to the Best Music for Kids!

*G*OOD MUSIC *B*RIGHTER CHILDREN

SIMPLE AND PRACTICAL IDEAS TO HELP TRANSFORM YOUR CHILD'S LIFE THROUGH THE POWER OF MUSIC

SHARLENE HABERMEYER

ISBN 0-7615-2150-X / Paperback
368 pages / U.S. $15.95 / Can. $23.50

PRIMA

To order, call (800) 632-8676 or
visit us online at www.primalifestyles.com

Turn Your Child into a *Great* Reader!

Are you concerned about your child's reading ability? Does your child hate to read? If so, you are not alone. In fact, 38 percent of American fourth graders are unable to read at a basic level. Now you can turn your nonreader child into a reading star—in just four to six months! Based on research done at Yale, this step-by-step guide for parents and teachers is packed with easy-to-read cartoons, games, and fun phonic sheets that make it easy to teach almost any child to read at or above grade level. With the simple steps outlined by reading expert Peggy Wilber, you'll discover how to:

- **Determine your child's specific reading needs**

- **Help your child develop comprehension strategies**

- **Enhance your child's phonic skills**

- **Improve your child's auditory skills**

- **Choose great reading selections at the right level for your child**

- **And much more!**

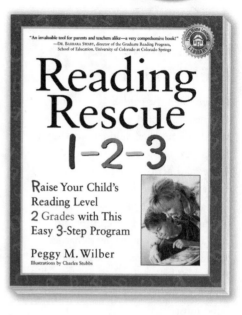

"An invaluable tool for parents and teachers alike—a very comprehensive book!"
—Dr. Barbara Swaby, director of the Graduate Reading Program, School of Education, University of Colorado at Colorado Springs

Reading Rescue 1-2-3

Raise Your Child's Reading Level 2 Grades with This Easy 3-Step Program

Peggy M. Wilber
Illustrations by Charles Stubbs

ISBN 0-7615-2963-2 / Paperback
272 pages / U.S. $16.00 / Can. $24.50

P
PRIMA

To order, call (800) 632-8676 or visit us online at www.primalifestyles.com